Education in the 80's:

SOCIAL STUDIES

Education in the 80's:

SOCIAL STUDIES

Jack Allen
Editor
George Peabody College for
Teachers of Vanderbilt University

Classroom Teacher Consultant
Carol J. Golden
Jackson and Whittier Elementary School
Everett, Washington

National Education Association
Washington, D.C.

Stock No. 3163–6–00 (paper)
        3164–4–00 (cloth)

Note

The opinions expressed in this publication should not be construed as representing the policy or position of the National Education Association. Materials published as part of the NEA Education in the 80's series are intended to be discussion documents for teachers who are concerned with specialized interests of the profession.

Acknowledgment

THIS LAND IS YOUR LAND, Words and music by Woody Guthrie; TRO–© Copyright 1956, 1958 and 1970 LUDLOW MUSIC, INC., New York, New York. Used by permission.

Library of Congress Cataloging in Publication Data
Main entry under title:

Education in the 80's.

  Includes bibliographical references.
  1. Social sciences—Study and teaching. I. Allen, Jack, 1941–
LB1584.E34   375'.3   80–24219
ISBN 0–8106–3164–4
ISBN 0–8106–3163–6 (pbk.)

Contents

Editor

Jack Allen, a past president of the National Council for the Social Studies, is the author of many textbooks and other instructional materials at the elementary and secondary levels. Dr. Allen is Professor of History Emeritus, George Peabody College for Teachers of Vanderbilt University.

Classroom Teacher Consultant

Carol J. Golden is a teacher in the Jackson and Whittier Elementary School, Everett, Washington.

What problems and challenges do today's students face during the 1980's? Such a question forces teachers and curriculum planners to rethink and reevaluate the rationale and content of instructional programs for the 80's. Current world problems, from turmoil in the Middle East to galloping inflation at home, compel teachers to provide instruction now that takes into consideration future societal needs.

This collection of articles edited by Jack Allen and published under the auspices of the National Education Association offers to the classroom teacher emphasis and direction for such future planning in social studies education. Included are chapters describing the purpose of social studies education; the use of both history and geography in teaching social studies; the inclusion of cultural pluralism as a humanistic dimension in social studies education; the changes in values brought about by an urbanized world; the importance of a global understanding of our world; the incorporation of basic skills instruction into a social studies program; and the teaching of values and the societal forces influencing values today. The information, opinions, and attitudes expressed in these articles can assist classroom teachers in determining what educational priorities are appropriate for students.

While some authors have included "how to" suggestions for teaching students various concepts such as the uneven distribution of limited resources, the complexity of world problems, and the importance of different viewpoints, most of the writing emphasizes the "why" and "what" of social studies programs. Importance is placed on readying students for sacrifices and changes in the near future and on helping them develop skills that will enable them to make wise choices in a world becoming more dependent on technology. Teachers are reminded of their important role as models and asked to examine their own values and behaviors.

Educators are interested in ensuring that students are taught those skills considered basic for coping in today's world. Although the full impact of the movement toward basic skills instruction is unclear, in some cases a shift toward such instruction can mean a shift away from social studies programs. What is more basic than developing informed and effective citizens? We must consider the consequences of long-term neglect of appropriate social studies education.

Acquiring the skills, knowledge, and values needed to make decisions, think critically, and cooperate with others must have high priorities in the 80's. A child should learn that the world is broader than his or her own neighborhood and that actions taken in one country can directly affect living conditions in another area of the world. Programs should help students clarify their feelings about newly acquired knowledge.

The final chapter of this book examines the role of the social studies teacher in the 80's. The author predicts that what will happen in programs for the social studies depends on teachers—teachers who are concerned and willing to do what is necessary to encourage students to recognize the importance of the individual in a world demanding cooperation. The classroom teacher who has read these articles will be better prepared to defend and promote social studies education as an essential part of any school's curriculum.

Carol J. Golden
Jackson and Whittier Elementary School
Everett, Washington

In 1939 a curriculum bulletin entitled *The Future of the Social Studies* was published by the National Council for the Social Studies. Edited by James A. Michener, who was at the time an active social studies educator, the bulletin was a collection of 15 different proposals for an experimental social studies curriculum, each put forth by a recognized leader in the field. In 1959, approximately two decades later, a Commission on the Social Studies of the same Council also considered the future, but in another manner. In a document entitled *Curriculum Planning in American Schools: The Social Studies,* the Commission studiously avoided recommending a specific curriculum design, electing instead to identify significant educational issues and provide a rationale for the planning of relevant programs. Now, another body of social studies educators again goes about the heady business of exploring the future.

This current monograph, developed under the auspices of the National Education Association, approaches the future—the 1980's—in a way somewhat different from either the 1939 or the 1958 statements. Like the 1939 bulletin, it employs a body of professionals, each functioning independently; like the 1958 report, it offers no specific grade-level proposals. But unlike either, its contributors approach the social studies from a variety of vantage points relative to goals, content, and strategies. Collectively, the contributions tend to be reflective rather than prescriptive. Mindful of the futurist axiom that unpredictability is the name of the game, they suggest emphases and directions. Readers in search of the key to a specific curriculum design may experience initial disappointment. But curricular implications abound. Moreover, they can either be identified with existing course arrangements and grade placement or be suggestive of new ways to fashion a scope and sequence.

The opening chapter speaks to the perennial question concerning the nature of social studies. Recognizing the presence of conflicting views and traditions, it diverts attention to purposes commonly held and implies that definitional differences, often vigorously expressed, may amount ultimately to little more than semantic quibbling. The second and third chapters perceive the social studies, in general terms, as two-dimensional. The former recognizes the assignment to social studies of the main responsibility for satisfying the citizenship education task in American schools. The latter affirms that the social studies also make a vital contribution to the humanistic experience.

A range of knowledge and understandings required by society, now and in the future, encompasses the subject matter of Chapters 4 through 8. The uses of the past at a time when technological innovations and global upheavals are revolutionizing human society, the physical realities of the stage on which the drama is being played—these historical and geographical ingredients are familiar social studies fare. Less hoary, but highly significant for the future, are three additional ingredients: cultural pluralism, as a phase of mounting interdependence; urbanization, as a process altering dramatically both societies and values; and global perspective, as an increasingly compelling requirement of modern life. In addition to these major knowledge ingredients, space limitations prevent attention to a number of laudable, and frequently more transitory emphases, such as law-related education, career education, and a host of others.

Skills especially endemic to social studies education are detailed in Chapters 9 and 10. Basic skills, particularly reading and writing, are examined in the former and include the firm admonition to teachers of social studies that they accept a proper share of responsibility for their development. Societal skills, such as decision making, are considered in Chapter 10, with emphasis placed on their essential role in effective social and civic action.

Values education as an integral component of social studies instruction is the subject of Chapter 11. Recognizing that values are the stuff of culture and being aware of the universality of cultural change, the role of the social studies in helping students clarify their values is seen as a paramount objective.

The larger society beyond the classroom has its own unique roles to play in social education. This is the message of Chapter 12. Educational forces, formal and informal, are continuously operative in a multimedia, interdependent world; they need to be recognized and understood by a citizenry, including educators, desirous of assessing the reliability and validity of social learning, in and out of school.

Confronted with the requirements of an unpredictable future, how are those who teach students to cope? The closing chapter examines this troublesome question. Predictably, it emphasizes the necessity for true educational professionals to regard their own education as an ongoing process. It insists that if teachers are to guide learners toward recognizable reality rather than some fanciful imaged past and present, they, too, must remain learners.

Jack Allen

CHAPTER 1

The Nature and Purposes of Social Studies

Charles L. Mitsakos

Some of the children who enter first grade in schools in the United States during the 1980's will graduate from colleges and universities and enter the work force after the year 2001. What these first graders learn between 1980 and 2001; what views they have of life in the new century; what knowledge, skills, and attitudes they acquire in their schools will determine their capacity for leadership and influence their personal happiness.

Many people would assume that these young women and men will be able to meet the problems of a new century in a new world. But will they be ready? This depends largely on whether schools prepare them for the world that is going, the twentieth century, or for the world that is coming. The one dimension of schooling that has prime responsibility in this regard is social studies education. The challenge before the schools is that—in the field of education in general, and the social studies in particular—the twenty-first century has already arrived.

DEFINING THE SOCIAL STUDIES

It is impossible to offer a single satisfactory definition of social studies within German schools . . . when discussing social studies in Germany, at least six different terms—"Sozialkunde," "Gemein-

schaftskunde," "soziale Studien," "politische Bildung," "Gesell-
schaftslehre," and "Geschichte/Politik"—may be used.

The confusion over terminology reflects the confusion that
besets other aspects of social studies. The different expressions that
stand for social studies indicate the absence of agreement in the
Federal Republic of Germany on the goals, content, structure, and
theoretical basis for social studies.[1]

Although the above is drawn from the opening of a report on social
studies in the Federal Republic of Germany, many social studies educators would say that it could be accurately applied to the United States
of America.

Three Views of Social Studies

Unlike other school subjects such as mathematics or science, one
finds that people in the field hold varying opinions on the nature and
purpose of social studies. The social studies in the United States are
often considered by social studies educators and theoreticians in three
distinctive ways: as the social sciences simplified for pedagogical purposes, as citizenship transmission, and as training in critical thinking.

The social sciences upon which social studies draws include anthropology, economics, geography, history, sociology, psychology, and
political science. John V. Michaelis and A. Montgomery Johnston are
among those who describe the relationship between the social studies
and the social sciences. They conclude that social studies draws most of
its content from the social sciences and that these concepts and generalizations are simplified and taught along with the methods of inquiry of
the social scientist. Curriculum planning in the social studies draws data
related to the democratic heritage as well as to society's values, problems, and changing conditions from the social sciences. In addition,
the social studies draw data from the social sciences for psychological
foundations of curriculum planning related to socialization, child
development, and other psychological–methodological aspects of instruction.[2]

Many schools across the country, as well as several textbook publishers, have substituted the term *social sciences* for social studies, referring
to the high school "social science teachers" or to the company's elementary "social science series." The ERIC clearinghouse in the field is called
ERIC ChESS, ERIC Clearinghouse for Social Studies/Social Science Education.

Others feel that the social studies are charged with transmitting our
cultural heritage. Citizenship transmission draws on those moral and
ethical values that are commonly accepted as basic elements in Ameri-

can life. There is usually a strong emphasis on history and concepts such as the free enterprise system. There is common acceptance of a body of knowledge that is required for a good citizen and an effort to transmit this knowledge.[3] George Weber and the Council for Basic Education feel strongly that the schools can effectively teach only our nation's history and geography and, therefore, should stick to the basics involved in passing on our cultural heritage. The behavioral sciences, they state, are too complex for elementary and secondary students; valuing and reflective inquiry have no business in the schools.[4]

Still others view social studies as being primarily concerned with reflective thinking or decision making. They trace their roots back to Socrates, Plato, and Thucydides, and feel that "facts from which no conclusion can be drawn are hardly worth knowing" and that the "mark of the good citizen is the quality of decisions which he (or she) reaches on public and private matters of social concern."[5]

Proponents of this viewpoint feel that students should be equipped with a strong base of factual information so that they can become effective decision makers since some decisions involve essentially matters of fact. Most decisions, however, involve values as well as facts. Students must have valuing skills if they are to consider the value assumptions involved in their interpretation of facts and of the moral and ethical questions they are trying to answer. Shirley H. Engle, the major proponent of reflective inquiry, states:

> If the quality of decision-making is to be the primary concern of social studies instruction. . . . we must not only provide the opportunity for decision-making but we must see to it that decisions are made in keeping with well known rules of science and logic and that students get practice in making their decisions.[6]

Perhaps the three theoretical views of the social studies are best summarized by Figure 1.[7]

As social studies moves through the 1980's, there needs to be a greater realization among theorists and specialists in the field that there is no dichotomy between citizenship transmission and good social science or between decision making and good social science. Students cannot become effective citizens in our rapidly changing and increasingly interdependent world unless they have a good understanding of some of the fundamental concepts of the social sciences drawn from their national and global heritage. In order to deal with the dynamics or changing nature of knowledge and to solve new problems or understand new developments in the future, they must also have effective analytical skills and perspectives.

FIGURE 1

THE THREE SOCIAL STUDIES TRADITIONS

	Social Studies Taught as Citizenship Transmission	Social Studies Taught as Social Science	Social Studies Taught as Reflective Inquiry
Purpose	Citizenship is best promoted by inculcating right values as a framework for making decisions.	Citizenship is best promoted by decision making based on mastery of social science concepts, processes, and problems.	Citizenship is best promoted through a process of inquiry in which knowledge is derived from what citizens need to know to make decisions and solve problems.
Method	Transmission: Transmission of concepts and values by such techniques as textbook, recitation, lecture, question and answer sessions, and structured problem-solving exercises.	Discovery: Each of the social sciences has its own method of gathering and verifying knowledge. Students should discover and apply the method that is appropriate to each social science.	Reflective Inquiry: Decision making is structured and disciplined through a reflective inquiry process which aims at identifying problems and responding to conflicts by means of testing insights.
Content	Content is selected by an authority interpreted by the teacher and has the function of illustrating values, beliefs, and attitudes.	Proper content is the structure, concepts, problems, and processes of both the separate and the integrated social science disciplines.	Analysis of individual citizen's values yields needs and interests which, in turn, form the basis for student self-selection of problems. Problems, therefore, constitute the content for reflection.

Student Perceptions of Social Studies

The nature and purpose of the social studies at times appear confusing to the intended audience: students. Polls conducted during the 1960's at Boston University[8] and by the Louis Harris organization[9] indicate that students find history, geography, and other social studies courses less interesting and more irrelevant than most other school subjects.

The curriculum activities of the 1970's have had some impact on student attitudes and on their perceptions of social studies. Elementary students participating in a project of the National Association of Elementary School Principals expressed a positive feeling about social studies in general and about the study of other nations and other peoples in particular.[10] In another recent study, students in high schools across the country indicated a positive view of social studies in comparison to other courses. These students felt that social studies made use of a wide range of learning materials and activities, and required more student decision making than most other courses.[11] In yet another survey, twice as many students felt that learning mathematics and English was much more important for entrance into their chosen occupation than was social studies; these students also perceived class work in social studies as less difficult than math or English. In order to improve the nature of social studies courses, students recommended that teachers require more drawing of conclusions from data, teach analytical skills, and give fair and adequate treatment to the study of minority groups and other cultures.[12]

The more positive interest in social studies may be related in part to the impact of the many curriculum project materials developed in the 1960's and implemented in the 1970's. Although their impact may not have been as tremendous as some had hoped and others allege, these materials have had a considerable effect on practices incorporated in social studies classes. This conclusion is justified based on reviews of impact studies by such noted social studies researchers as Carole Hahn, Thomas Switzer, Frances Haley, and others. One is also struck by the impact of the new social studies when comparing the commercial textbooks and other available materials of 20 years ago with those being published today.[13] Students have had access to different instructional materials that may have resulted in their more positive views of social studies.

MAKING SOME BASIC ASSUMPTIONS

In contrast to the 1960's and 1970's, however, new curriculum development at a national level has been almost nonexistent in the 1980's. In addition, it does not appear that there will be a major influx of federal and/or foundation funds for this purpose. As schools examine their programs, adopt new texts, and revise their curriculums, they will have to look to other sources for guidance. It is essential that a framework that embraces a set of assumptions on the nature and purpose of social studies education be used both to assess existing programs and to evaluate new program options. The revised curriculum guidelines of the National Council for the Social Studies are based on the history and research in the field; they provide for a blend of citizenship training, good social science, and the effective development of decision making and of data gathering and data processing skills. The guidelines are sensitive to the needs and interests of students and to the real world of the classroom teacher. Originally developed in 1971, revised in light of experience with them in the schools, and updated to represent current research and development, the guidelines can serve as an effective blueprint for the 1980's.

An adapted version of the guidelines is presented below. The official NCSS position statement includes a rationale; an overview of the role of knowledge, abilities, valuing, and social participation in the social studies; and the nine major guidelines, accompanied by 74 standards delineating the guidelines as well as by suggestions on how to use the guidelines for social studies needs assessment.[14]

Guidelines for the 1980's

1. *Social studies programs for the 1980's should be directly related to the age, maturity, and concerns of students.*

   Programs should take into account the aptitudes and needs of the learners and provide all students with formal social studies experiences at all grade levels from kindergarten through high school. Provision should be made for student input into the formulation of goals, the selection of instructional materials, the identification of areas of concern for study, and the assessment of the program.

2. *Social studies programs for the 1980's should deal with the real social world.* Programs should focus on the world as it really is with its strengths, problems, and promises; build upon the realities of the immediate school community; and provide opportunities for analysis and attempts to formulate potential resolutions of local and global issues and problems. Active participation in the real social world should be considered an integral element of the program, as should the opportunity for students to work with members of racial, ethnic, and national groups other than their own.

3. *Social studies programs for the 1980's should draw from currently valid knowledge representative of human experience, culture, and beliefs.*

Programs should develop important and valid concepts drawn from all of the social sciences, as well as from related fields; they should represent a balance between Western and non-Western cultures, among the nation's ethnic and racial groups, among the local, national, and global concerns, and among the past, present, and future. Proficiency in gathering and processing information (inquiry and decision-making skills) should be developed.

4. *Objectives of social studies programs for the 1980's should be carefully selected and clearly stated in such form as to furnish direction to the programs.* Knowledge, abilities, valuing, and social participation should be represented in objectives that are carefully formulated in light of what is known about the students, the real social world, and the content fields of knowledge. Instructional objectives should call for students to develop all aspects of the affective, cognitive, and psychomotor domains through learning activities that are appropriate and clearly focused.

5. *Learning activities of social studies programs for the 1980's should engage students directly and actively in the learning process.*
   Programs should provide students with a rich set of learning activities that includes practicing methods of inquiry, examining values, and making decisions. These varied and flexible experiences, ranging from studying texts and reading poetry to participating in discussions and making field trips, should directly involve the students. Students should be encouraged to investigate and respond to the human condition in the contemporary world. Learning must go on in an atmosphere of trust and sensitivity to individual rights.

6. *Strategies of instruction and learning activities of social studies programs for the 1980's should rely on a broad range of learning resources.*
   Programs should draw upon a variety of media that are selected carefully to meet the wide range of interests, needs, and abilities of the students and to relate directly to the objectives. Classroom activities should use the school and the community as learning laboratories, and draw upon community resource persons and organizations that provide students with some primary sources representing many points of view and a mix of cultures.

7. *Social studies programs for the 1980's must facilitate the organization of experience.*

The structure of social studies programs must help students organize their experiences in such a manner that they will learn how to continue to learn, see relationships, and apply their learned concepts and skills in order to solve future problems.

8. *Evaluation of social studies programs for the 1980's should be useful, systematic, comprehensive, and valid for the objectives of the programs.*
   Regular assessment of student progress in the program should come from many sources, such as pencil-and-paper tests, anecdotal records, and role playing, and should measure achievement in content knowledge as well as in such skills and abilities as critical thinking, valuing, and social participation. Evaluation should be both formative, contributing to the development of the program and/or student progress, and summative, contributing to the overall terminal success of the program and/or student.

9. *Social studies education for the 1980's should receive vigorous support as a vital and responsible part of the school program.*
   School administrators, teachers, boards of education, and the community have a responsibility to actively support social studies programs by providing appropriate instructional time, materials, consultant services, and facilities; by encouraging innovation and social participation; and by preserving academic freedom. Teachers must be active in curriculum development and assessment, and participate regularly in such activities as workshops, courses, reading, travel, and professional association programs.

SUMMARY

This opening chapter has examined the nature and purpose of the social studies. It has reviewed the search for a precise definition and focus by social studies theorists, teachers, and students. A brief synopsis of a set of standards relating to the nature and purpose of the social studies has been provided.

The 1980's offer the prospect of a vitality in the social studies that may be realized through the implementation of standards that are based on a strong set of assumptions about the nature and purpose of the field —standards that will make the field intellectually honest and rewarding to its proponents and interesting and relevant to its clientele. Only then will social studies education be capable of meeting society's challenge for today's students: to develop informed citizens for the twenty-first

QUERENCIA[2]

Querencia is a Spanish term meaning the affection one feels for the place one calls home and the sense of well-being one derives from that place. *Querencia* is the feeling of contentment that people experience when they know they are where they belong.

Ordinarily, people find their *querencia* in very limited environments: home, neighborhood, town, or city. Yet *querencia* seems infinitely expansive. Some have such feelings about particular regions of the country. Travel-weary Americans, returning from trips abroad, may experience *querencia* upon landing in the United States. Astronauts have expressed their sense of attachment to the bluish-green orb called Earth as they have gazed upon it from outer space. Apparently, the way to feel *querencia* most keenly is to leave "home"—however that is defined—and cope for a time in a strange environment.

Querencia is an emotional feeling that is difficult to explain. Why does an old man released from prison after many years of internment choose to return to his cell rather than to cope with the complexities of freedom? Why does a Russian emigré, forced out of the U.S.S.R. because of her political beliefs, long to return? Literature and music offer hundreds of examples, but few explanations, of the deep attachment people acquire for their homes.

Nationalism tries to convert this natural affection for home into loyalty to the nation–state, its ideology, its form of government, and, on occasion, even its political leaders. The achievements that have resulted from nationalism are well known; so, too, are the crimes committed against mankind on behalf of zealous patriotism and ultranationalism.

Despite abuses, *querencia*—the feeling that one belongs, is part of society, and has a stake in it—is essential for modern citizenship, at least in a democracy. Much citizenship behavior depends upon voluntary compliance. Paying taxes, obeying traffic laws, practicing tolerance toward others, and countless other civic acts require individuals to act civilly without coercion. Moreover, to lack *querencia* is to be alienated, to feel like a stranger in society. The alienated take little or no interest in public affairs and are unwilling to participate. They may not feel bound to observe the subtle rules that hold a society together. In extreme cases the alienated may even take delight in watching the society crumble. Thus, not only is *querencia* a part of citizenship but also it is probably a precondition for other aspects of citizenship education.

Many educators appear uncomfortable with the affective side of citizenship. Perhaps, some recall the loyalty oaths of the 1950's and the limits that were placed upon free speech in classrooms. Others recoil at mindless recitations of "pledges of allegiance" or courses aimed at promoting the "blessings of democracy and the evils of communism." Still others, disillusioned by the gap between American political ideals and some of its practices, have grown cynical about political life.

Despite the justifiable restraints these and other factors may place on the willingness of some teachers to promote the affective elements of citizenship, we must realize that effective citizenship cannot survive in a climate of despair. Citizenship demands commitment, and teachers must help youth make commitments. Such commitments should not take the form of blind devotion. Those who feel *querencia* are usually aware of the blemishes and inadequacies of the home they treasure. They love it anyway for its strengths and in spite of its imperfections, and they seek to improve it as best they can. But to expect citizen engagement without commitment is unrealistic.

Nearly all children appear at the school door with some manifestation of *querencia*. It is not the teacher's job to destroy this feeling or to change it substantially. Rather, the public correctly expects teachers to encourage it, to extend it, and to make it the basis for positive citizen action.

POLITISCHE BILDUNG

Politische bildung is a German term. It may be translated as "political education," but its German use is different from its American one. For many Americans, political education connotes political indoctrination, promotion of one political party over another, or support of a particular faction's political policies. For Germans, political education refers to the provision of the knowledge and skills that one needs to function politically in a complex, democratic society. To Germans, political education means education for citizenship.

It might be useful to review the German situation. In 1945 the Germans surrendered to the Allies following the most destructive war in history. The German nation was divided, stripped of its resources, and disgraced in the eyes of most of the world. Those living in the Federal Republic of Germany would soon experience their fourth *form* of government in less than 50 years. An earlier effort at democratic government, the Weimar Republic, failed to find roots in Germany and fell easy prey to the Nazis. After 1933 vast numbers of Germans enthusiastically supported a popular, charismatic leader who ultimately led the nation to destruction. Acts committed in the name of Germany horrified the world and left a sense of guilt that would afflict future generations of Germans who could not be held accountable. In 1945 the German people lacked pride in their nation; they felt shame for its deeds and contempt for their political leaders.

The political goals of the Allied Occupation Forces were to root out any remaining vestiges of fascism and to build a base for a democratic government. But how was this to be done in the presence of limited experience with democracy, a political culture that seemed hostile to democracy, and extensive apathy? Programs were mounted to teach people about democracy and to interest them in public issues. Later "centers for political education" were established in each of the länder and at the federal level. Political education was beamed over television, was promoted by unions and management, found its way into popular journals and newspapers, and appeared in the school curriculum. Germany undertook a massive program to train people in the essentials of democracy—and it succeeded.

Nothing quite so dramatic and far-reaching is needed in the United States. We do not have a political culture that is hostile to democracy. Yet, direct, self-conscious political education is as essential here as it was in Germany. While children acquire their political attitudes mainly outside of school, the knowledge and a majority of the skills they need to understand and participate in the political system are best learned in school. To withhold political education is to deny a child his or her birthright as an American citizen. To ignore political education is also to threaten the future of democracy in America.

There is not sufficient space in this essay to discuss all of the knowledge and skills that students require in order to fill the citizen role adequately, but some examples may help make the point. At a minimum, students require knowledge of the institutions and structure of American government, the principles upon which the American system is based, the political processes that affect the operation of the institutions, and some of the enduring political issues that confront the American public.

Knowledge of the Institutions and Structure of American Government. Students need to understand what it means to live in a republic, operated as a federal system, under rules set forth by a constitution. They must comprehend the relationships among the three branches of government and how these branches can "check and balance" each other. They should fathom the relationships between state governments and the federal government, and the relationships between local units of government and the states.

Knowledge of the Principles of the American Political System. Students must go beyond simple recognition of the term *democracy* and the principles of freedom enunciated in the Bill of Rights. One study after another has documented that students can verbalize slogans about these principles and others, but they are frequently unable to apply them to concrete situations. Indeed, confronted with highly controversial situations, they sometimes choose antidemocratic solutions that violate fundamental freedoms.

Knowledge of Political Processes. It is not enough for students to comprehend the principles of the American political system and the institutions of government. They must also understand politics—the informal processes that make the entire system work. Currently students probably know less about politics than they do about the structure of government. They are taught the "steps" by which a bill becomes a law, but they are not told about the ways in which various pressure groups influence legislation at multiple points in the legislative process. Students learn that a President must seek the "advice and consent" of the Senate before a treaty can take effect, but they learn little or nothing about the political process involved in winning each Senator's support.

Knowledge of Enduring Political Issues. Students need to be informed about some of the enduring political issues that face government. For example, to what degree should the government serve as a balance wheel for the economy, ensuring that wealth is not skewed unduly to the few, regulating prices and protecting the consumer, propping up unsuccessful enterprises, and underwriting American business expansion? To what extent should the federal government guarantee that the rights and privileges enjoyed by certain groups in one or more states become available to similar groups in all states? How far should the government go in trying to make the ladder of success equally accessible to all? The details of these and many other issues change from month to month and year to year, but the fundamental issues remain the same and should be understood by all citizens.

Negotiation Skill. There are many political skills students should acquire. Only one—the skill of negotiation—will be treated here. The act of politics is largely the act of bargaining. People with competing goals enter the political arena to find solutions that will at least partially satisfy everyone. The usual goal is not to have winners and losers, but to have everyone win a little. One of the politicians' most important skills is to find the solution that attracts the largest possible amount of support. Political decisions that lack such support are rarely effective. Lack of understanding of the bargaining process and of the necessity for compromise is one of the reasons naive Americans hold politicians in low esteem. And their own lack of bargaining skill is a factor that

26

prevents many Americans from becoming more successful politically.

No teacher can assume realistically that teaching political knowledge and skills will make all students equally active political participants. A person's sense of *querencia* is a controlling factor. Those who feel alienated are unlikely to participate fully, no matter what knowledge or skills they possess. Personality is important. Some political activities reward forceful, outgoing personalities. The shy are less likely to run for office than are the extroverts. Time and energy play a role. Most people must work for a living and care for their families. Personal and family concerns typically outweigh political ones. Only a small minority ever become full-time political activists. But everyone deserves the knowledge necessary to become aware of political happenings and to interpret them properly. And all citizens should possess the skills that enable them to take action effectively, when they choose to, on issues important to them. The schools owe this, at least, to their students.

SOCIAL STUDIES

Social studies is an American term. It refers to a portion of the elementary and secondary school curriculum set aside to teach students about the relationship of human beings to their social and physical environment. Although it is organized variously from state to state and from school district to school district, it usually contains data, concepts, generalizations, and modes of inquiry based upon such academic disciplines as anthropology, economics, geography, history, philosophy, political science, psychology, and sociology. Social studies is distinguished from these academic disciplines by the overriding concern of social studies teachers to organize their instruction and select their content so as to provide a sound citizenship education for their students.

The social studies curriculum is not solely responsible for the citizenship education of youth. The media, especially television, are a more powerful source of information about current happenings in politics. Parents, churches, and peer groups are a greater influence on student attitudes. Other school subjects provide some of the knowledge and skills students require to play their citizen role well. And extracurricular activities provide opportunities to practice citizenship in controlled settings.

Nevertheless, social studies teachers have unique and special opportunities to enhance the citizenship education of youth. Social studies courses are a major source of information about political life in the United States and in other countries. Students can read about the activities of past political leaders. They can study the principles upon which

the nation was founded and observe how politics really works. Social studies classes can provide forums for students to discuss current public issues and to try out ideas for how such issues can be best resolved. The classroom can be a place where students can hone the skills necessary for effective political participation.

Roles of Social Studies Teachers. Social studies teachers fill at least three roles as citizenship educators: They are role models of an ideal citizen, instructors in citizenship, and coordinators of out-of-classroom resources for citizenship education.

Whether they want the role or not, teachers serve as role models of the ideal citizen. It is true that the models they project will have a differential impact on their students. For young students who lack strong adult role models at home, the impact may be tremendous. For older youth, especially those who have already found effective models, the consequences may be less. Nevertheless, teachers cannot forget that what they are and how they act are as important as what they say. By their own interest in politics, by their participation in political activities, and by their willingness to show commitment, they indicate that politics is important and that students should also become engaged. Through their capacity to criticize and judge fairly the acts of public officials and through their attempts to offer constructive countersolutions, they exhibit the traits of a reflective citizen. And by their own behavior before the class—treating students equitably, respecting their views, and responding in a just and fair manner to classroom problems —teachers set standards to which all can aspire.

Social studies teachers have a responsibility to encourage the growth of citizenship attitudes, knowledge, and skills in whatever subjects they teach. Some courses—particularly American government, civics, problems of democracy, and American history—are especially appropriate for citizenship education. But elementary school social studies, and even high school courses in world geography, economics, and sociology, provide occasions for instruction about citizenship if teachers will exploit them.

Teachers should also be alert to new ideas relating to particular aspects of citizenship education that they can incorporate within existing courses. For example, advocates of "law-related education" stress the importance of law in American society and the need to teach students about the fundamental principles of American government. Proponents of global education have expanded the concept of citizenship worldwide, inviting teachers to conceive of Earth as a "global village." Those specializing in moral education and values education encourage teachers to help students address the ethical consequences of

28

their decisions and the impact these decisions have on society. Advocates of political behavior draw attention to the factors that influence how people behave and point out the informal processes of government. And champions of political participation suggest ways in which students can begin to put their knowledge of politics to work in the school and the community. These and other groups enrich the range of resources available for citizenship education in schools. But the decision as to how to combine these ideas with more traditional ones—or even whether to use them all—remains, as it has always been, one for teachers to make for themselves.

The third role teachers can fill is that of coordinator for out-of-class resources for citizenship education. Political attitudes, knowledge, and skills should not remain inert abstractions. They ought to be put into practice, both in school and in the community the school serves. School clubs, the student council, advisory committees to the principal, and other settings provide opportunities for students to contribute to the political life of the school and to practice what they have learned in class. Through volunteering for activities in the community and participating in political campaigns, students can gain experience and develop their sense of *querencia* at the same time. If these opportunities are to be exploited, however, it requires teachers who are willing to devote time to planning and coordinating them.

CONCLUSION

It is important to keep this simple fact in mind: There is no natural law or heavenly edict that self-government must survive in the United States. The founders established it; the members of each new generation must recommit themselves to its goals or it will perish. The defense of democracy is more than a willingness to bear arms against foreign invaders. Democracy is defended every day in social studies classrooms when teachers help students understand its principles and accept the responsibility of citizenship.

There is no greater purpose in education than the cultivation of good citizenship. There is no greater heritage to leave to young people than the capacity to govern themselves in enlightened self interest.

REFERENCES

1. We are grateful to the Danforth Foundation for providing the support that has made possible this article and other activities undertaken on behalf of citizenship education.

2. We learned about *querencia* from "The Talk of the Town." *The New Yorker* Magazine, September 26, 1977. p. 27.

CHAPTER 3

Social Studies: The Humanistic Dimension

Jack Allen

Consider the probing observation of American architect–philosopher Louis H. Sullivan, the late nineteenth century prophet of modern architecture:

> Must I then specify? Must I show you this French chateau . . . here in New York, and still you do not laugh! Must you wait until you see a modern man come out of its door, before you laugh? Have you no sense of humor, no sense of pathos? Must I then explain to you that, while the man may live in the house physically, he cannot live in it morally, mentally or spiritually, that he and his house are a paradox? That he himself is an illusion when he believes his chateau to be real . . . ?[1]

Reflect on the actions and feelings of American painter Grant Wood as he achieved recognition and notoriety in the 1920's and 1930's. Having saved enough money teaching in public school, Wood left the familiar surroundings of the Iowa heartland and journeyed to Paris in search of inspiration. Conforming to the accepted Parisian mode, he nurtured a pinkish beard, parted in the middle, and donned a Basque beret. Such affectations, however, did nothing to help his painting. In despair, he returned to his native Iowa, shaved off his beard, exchanged his beret for a pair of overalls, and concluded that he really got his best ideas "while milking a cow."

Listen to the words and music of contemporary American folk artist Woody Guthrie, as he sings:

This land is your land, this land is my land
From California to the New York island
From the redwood forest to the gulf stream waters;
This land was made for you and me!©[2]

Puzzle at the wonder of the Angkor remains where the Khmer peoples devoted their energies for six centuries to the building of a galaxy of magnificent temples, only, for reasons still awaiting adequate explanation, to steal away unobtrusively, leaving their handiwork to be consumed by the Cambodian jungle. . . . Or observe a modern Japanese family as it lights its candles before a Shinto shrine. . . . Or relate to English activist Thomas Paine, voice of the American War for Independence, as he affirmed, "The World is my country, all mankind are my brethren, and to do good is my religion." . . . Or empathize with a bewildered array of Vietnamese boat people as they flee the ravages of their homeland and face the uncertain prospects of a voyage at sea and the search for a future dwelling place. . . .

Each of the foregoing speaks to the humanistic dimension of social studies. Each is a manifestation of the humanistic experience. All exemplify members of the human family responding to circumstances of the moment or living out their lives in ways that may or may not be subject to their ultimate control. All have relevance for the teaching–learning process as today's students seek their own means of self-identification and their future courses of action.

TWO DIMENSIONS OF SOCIAL STUDIES

Social studies, viewed in general perspective, may be thought of as two-dimensional. For purposes of self-realization, social studies contribute to the humanistic experience. To help realize the goals of a democratic society that derives its just powers from the consent of the governed, the social studies program serves as an agency for citizenship education. If the former purpose is individualistic, the latter is collectivistic. But the duality of purpose symbolized by the configuration is, in truth, a gestalt. The two purposes are largely inseparable. Effectively oriented personality development contributes to good citizenship practices. Popular government and a humane social order are enhanced by a citizenry that finds fulfillment and security in both leadership and followship roles. Humanistic learnings can provide a sense of appropri-

31

ate involvement in either type of situation. Concomitantly, the humanistic experience may function with equal force in noncivic enterprises and nonvocational endeavors, as, for instance, in the realization of personal desires and actions typically associated with the ways of a leisure society.

THE NATURE OF THE HUMANISTIC EXPERIENCE

The humanistic experience is fundamentally concerned with the human spirit. Its basic values are, in the words of O.B. Hardison, "the free play of the mind and, its corollary, an expanded sense of self in its relation to the world."[3] Accordingly, excessive efforts to politicize or categorize it should be resisted. Equally relevant, the humanistic experience deals not only with the rich and powerful but also with the ordinary people and the most common aspects of everyday life. It listens, attentively, to the voices of poets and peasants; it analyzes, with equal diligence, the machinations of saints and sinners; it observes, thoughtfully, both the fountains and the ash heaps of human society. In short, the world is its oyster.

In a more legalistic vein, the humanistic experience has received expression in the congressional act that established, in 1965, the National Endowment for the Humanities. The legislation defined "humanities" as including, but not limited to, the study of "language, both modern and classical; linguistics; literature; history; jurisprudence; philosophy; archeology; comparative religion; ethics; the history, criticism, theory, and practice of the arts; those aspects of the social sciences which have humanistic content and employ humanistic methods." Clearly, a definition so comprehensive in scope embodies innumerable relationships and linkages with programs in the social studies.

THE PRACTICALITY OF HUMANISTIC LEARNING

Given the association of humanistic learning with social studies programs, questions remain: Is humanistic learning practical? Is it part of what is truly basic in the educative process? For the pragmatic American, the marketplace has a certain primacy, the responsibilities of a collective citizenry a fundamental imperative. And these, indeed, are legitimate concerns. The problem is to place them within the context of the contemporary world, a world that could possibly be in the midst of the most revolutionary period in human history. Consider a few of the prevailing winds of change: an urbanized world rapidly gaining ascendancy over the ways of the traditional rural, pastoral society; an automated technology symbolized by the microelectronics revolution, speeding the demise of the industrial, as well as the agricultural, worker; instantaneous worldwide communication coupled with accelerating means of transportation; and increasing global requirements for shared resources and shared knowledge.[4]

In these revolutionary times, the educative process speaks, with an ever louder and more resounding voice, in support of John Dewey's credo of a nonstatic education for a nonstatic world. It listens with increased attention to Whitehead's warning of the dangers inherent in an education designed to produce fixed persons for fixed duties. Schooling becomes a matter of providing environments in which individuals and groups can learn more efficiently and effectively.

In terms of the work force, the product of such environments is what Peter Drucker calls the "knowledge worker."[5] This type of worker performs tasks cooperatively, aware of the institution as a whole and not simply managed by strict hierarchical decisions. The consequence for such an individual is a sense of personal satisfaction that derives not only from the finished product or well-performed service but also from the feeling of having participated in the institution's role in society. This more cooperative mode, in what Daniel Bell identifies as post-industrial society, is, to Bell, "more difficult than the management of things."[6] It demands of the knowledge worker both productive labor and continuous learning.

Beyond the requirements of the marketplace, the new society makes apparent the need for increased attention to education for leisure. It calls for humanistic learning that defines leisure in the Greek or Aristotelian sense as freedom from work rather than as a contrived opportunity for recreation. It is, moreover, education with an existential flavor, recognizing that individuals in an urbanized, technologically oriented society, confronted with varieties of organizational restraints, need to learn increasingly to live within themselves.[7]

APPLICATIONS TO THE SOCIAL STUDIES CURRICULUM

The humanistic experience has applications across the total scope and sequence of the school curriculum. Within the social studies, it can take innumerable forms. For purposes of illustration, consider a variety of humanistic applications made at progressive maturity levels and formulated within the context of a prevailing social studies curriculum sequence.

Social studies for young children seeks to help the learner develop a sense of self, an awareness of the person in relation to the group.

Examined for this purpose are methods of communicating, working, and playing. There is, likewise, the quest for a sense of community, a sense of one's self in a community setting. Here, the young child views simple proposals for achieving authentic community in terms of the values of a good life and an awareness of the physical design of community.

Older children, in their social studies experiences, are brought in touch with the individual's relationship to one's total environment: the physical earth; basic human needs; resources required to meet needs. Learners place the relationship in historical perspective through probings into the American past and through speculations as to how this past impacts on contemporary society. They are also brought into contact with the nature of culture past and present, on a global scale, as they pursue cultural manifestations in terms of the values and ways of both simple and complex societies.

A sense of self acquires new meanings for young adolescents as they move out of childhood and go about the potentially traumatic task of severing traditional ties with the family group and a restrictive environmental setting. The function of the social studies comes in helping members of this age group see themselves in relation to such things as ethnic origins, kinship networks, local group ties, and identifiable subcultures. Adolescent students may do this by, say, examining the late twentieth century American household, with its clearly divided sex roles and marked separation of home and work environments. And they might pursue comparable matters in historical terms: for instance, the seasonal rhythms of Native Americans disrupted by the expansion of white settlement; the social and psychological impact on young women workers of their movement in the early nineteenth century from rural surroundings to burgeoning mill towns; the subtle forms of slave resistance to planter decrees.

For older adolescents and young adults, applications of the humanistic experience to the social studies offer rich potential in terms of both procedures and learnings. The following are a few suggestions related to approach and content:

1. Use of oral history with newly arrived persons from other countries to explore crosscultural similarities and differences and varying historical traditions;

2. Examination of specific problems in contemporary American culture and some of the social and psychological factors that give rise to them;

3. Analysis of forms of alienation in the modern technological society, viewed globally;

4. Study of various art forms—painting, architecture, music, imaginative literature, etc.—as manifestations of culture.

NATIONAL HUMANITIES PROJECTS

Beyond the bounds of formal schooling, and outside the realm of the typical social studies classroom, support for humanistic activities and projects is being generated across the nation. Especially notable in this regard is the leadership provided by the National Endowment for the Humanities. An independent, federal grantmaking agency, the Endowment supports projects of research, education, and public activity. Its stated purposes reveal much that can be of interest to those involved with education in the social studies:

1. To promote the public understanding of the humanities and their value in thinking about the current conditions of national life.

2. To improve the quality of teaching in the humanities and its responsiveness to new intellectual currents and changing social concerns.

3. To strengthen the scholarly foundation of humanistic study, and to support research activity that enriches the life of the mind in America.

4. To nurture the future well-being of those essential institutional and human resources that make possible the study of the humanities.

One program of the National Endowment, begun in 1972 and of particular relevance for education in social studies, is Youthgrants in the Humanities. Designed for young persons in their teens and twenties, the program makes grants for independent projects to benefit the community, the general public, or other young people. By the close of the 1970's, more than 500 Youthgrants had been awarded in all 50 states to recipients ranging in age from 13 to 30. A small sample of successful projects illustrates how the interest and ingenuity of young people find expression in realizable ways:

1. An eighth grader in historic Newburgh, New York, became concerned that the town's strange and beautiful old houses were rapidly being torn down. After studying old records in the public library and talking with a local restoration architect, the student made photographs and developed a slide show for

Newburgh citizens that aroused fresh interest in the preservation of these historic treasures.

2. A group of 20 teen-agers in the Black History Club of the Chicago Better Boy's Foundation developed *A Study of the Underground Railroad in Illinois,* a booklet on the fugitive slave system. Following documentary research and interviews with local scholars, the booklet was produced and made available to the Chicago public schools.

3. Two young Oregon cinematographers who were interested in the historical romance of the Willamette River produced a half-hour film depicting nineteenth-century life along this Northwest stream. The film, developed with the aid of diaries, interviews, old photos, and period maps, was scored with folk music of the era. It elicited great interest among schools, colleges, and civic groups in the region.

Another type of national effort that, in some respects, more specifically illustrates the melding of humanistic and citizenship goals is the Great American Achievements Program. Sponsored by the Bicentennial Council of the Thirteen Original States Fund, Inc., this program defines its task as follows: "to keep before the American people the vital meaning of those principles, ideals and values on which this Republic was founded—as well as the application of those evolving precepts to our nation's present-day social, political and economic problems." To achieve this purpose, the Great American Achievements Program has been involved, since 1977, in a 13-year re-evaluation of the Revolutionary Era through study of themes or concepts that subsume the fabric of our government. Each year a Commemorative Conference brings together some 200 opinion leaders from national, state, and community organizations to examine and interpret the historical and present-day meaning of a particular theme—One Nation Indivisible (1977); A New Republic Among Nations (1978); Of, By, and For the People (1979); Education for a Free People (1980); etc. The Council plans to culminate its 13-year effort in 1989 with due recognition of the 200th anniversary of the ratification of the U.S. Constitution.[8]

A VIEW OF THE FUTURE

Since 1779 when Thomas Jefferson, in proposing a law to establish public schools in Virginia, called "the people . . . the only safe depositories" of government, the social studies, by whatever name, have been vested with responsibilities for citizenship education. Perhaps less explicitly across these two centuries, the social studies have also maintained a humanistic dimension. Without denigrating the citizenship responsibility, the nature of modern society provides compelling arguments for clearly delineated humanistic experiences at all levels in the social studies program. Such experiences are, and will become, increasingly useful to the individual as a knowledge worker, a leisure recipient, and an integrated personality. And, while social studies is assuredly only one of a number of programmatic areas involved with humanistic learnings, it is a curricular domain that has much to offer as the citizenry peers anxiously into an unpredictable, revolutionary future.

REFERENCES

1. Sullivan, Louis H. *Kindergarten Chats.* New York: Wittenborn, Schultz, Inc., 1947. (Quoted in Handlin, Oscar. *Readings in American History.* New York: Alfred A. Knopf, 1957. p. 446.)

2. Acknowledgment: THIS LAND IS YOUR LAND, Words and music by Woody Guthrie; TRO-© Copyright 1956, 1958 and 1970 LUDLOW MUSIC, INC., New York, New York. Used by permission.

3. Hardison, O.B. *Toward Freedom and Dignity: The Humanities and the Idea of Humanity.* Baltimore: Johns Hopkins University Press, 1972. p. 26.

4. Allen, Jack. "The Revolution of Our Time." *Issue Today.* Teachers edition. Vol. 2, No. 15. Middletown, Conn.: American Education Publications, 1970. p. 1. (See also: Osborne, Adam. *Running Wild: The Next Industrial Revolution.* Berkeley, Calif.: Osborne/McGraw-Hill, Inc., 1979.

5. Drucker, Peter. *Management.* New York: Harper and Row, 1973. p. 177.

6. Bell, Daniel. *The Cultural Contradictions of Capitalism.* New York: Basic Books, Inc., 1976.

7. Allen, Jack. *loc. cit.*

8. One outgrowth of the Annual Commemorative Conferences is the preparation of study kits for schools and community groups. For example, a study kit based on the 1977 conference theme consists of a theme book by J.R. Pole, *The Idea of Union;* a conference volume by Jack Allen, *One Nation Indivisible: An Analysis of Unity Throughout American History;* and an audiovisual component, *One Nation Indivisible.* Further information about the Great American Achievements Program can be obtained by writing to The Bicentennial Council of the Thirteen Original States Fund, Inc., 901 North Washington Street, Suite 300, Alexandria, Virginia 22314.

CHAPTER 4

The Uses of History

Richard E. Gross

A variety of reasons has been put forward by natural and social scientists, as well as by philosophers and religionists, for the existence of the qualities of humanness that characterize men and women and that separate us from the beasts. One key element that is sometimes overlooked in such lists is humankind's unique ability to communicate across time. History—his and her story—was originally expressed orally and artistically; it began to take written form only a little over 5,000 years ago. Ever since, we have been able to employ this medium to pass on between generations vital knowledge, cherished affirmations, myths, and dreams, as well as traditions and other bases for the further extension of culture and civilization. At the heart of this process is history —an explanation of what has happened to humankind and how we came to be as we are, where we are, today.

HISTORY—ITS USE AND MISUSE

Through the years the study and writing of history gradually became a discipline in its own right. In the West the Greek writers in the era before Christ, such as Herodotus and Thucydides, came to be identified as "fathers" of history. During the ensuing centuries, historical content found its way into education as part of the Seven Liberal Arts and Scripture study, but it was not until the 1500's and 1600's that history emerged as a school subject in its own right. Indeed, in many countries today history does not have as important a place in the curriculum as it tends to have in the United States.

Eventually history was used by leaders—both reactionary kings trying to certify their rule and revolutionaries anxious to justify their actions—as propaganda, as a means of indoctrination for their causes. It is unfortunate that much of history has been so twisted and misapplied to fit certain points of view. However, such misshaping has been easy to accomplish because history does not exist fully and correctly between the covers of any tome. Most of the past is undocumented. It is estimated that we know less than 1 percent of the totality of human history. Numerous events, even in the recent past, are clouded by the lack of confirming evidence and by conflicting data and viewpoints.

A major challenge to all teachers is to help children and youth come to understand that, at its best, history is an incomplete account and a partial explanation of unique events in humankind's past that is created by the work and judgment of historians. We must help our students recognize that what often appears in conventional textbooks as uncontested truth is really an author's interpretation influenced by a variety of factors, any one of which might easily alter the explanation of both how and why something occurred, as well as the very description of the event itself. Early in their elementary schooling, pupils should be introduced to conflicting accounts and viewpoints. One of the best ways to do this is by involving them in roles as reporters of events; as such, they can observe and provide as accurate and complete descriptions as possible, with each description including the who's, what's, when's, where's, why's, and how's of the given happening.

MAJOR CONTRIBUTIONS OF HISTORY

Any discipline needs to provide particular contributions to knowledge and to society if it is to remain a viable and distinct instrument and entity. Within the limitations indicated previously, history still makes two such fundamental offerings: First, it does provide us with at least a partial mirror of our past, with a background that makes the present at least somewhat comprehensible; second, history has its own method, its own way of ascertaining as exactly as possible the factors contributing to an event, a series of developments, or a movement that is being traced. Other contributions are frequently cited on behalf of history—e.g., providing a means of generalizing about human behavior, a guide to the future, a contribution to good citizenship, a basis for national loyalty, a reservoir of culture, a source of understanding and compassion for other peoples, etc. None of the foregoing, however, is unique to history, and each can lead to error and misapplication. The problem for teachers and the schools is the fact that these supplementary goals for history instruction loom large in the overall role of the social studies and also in the calendar for public education.

The conflict for the teacher and the school lies in deciding on the place and the uses of history within the social studies and civic education programs. It would seem that a balance is called for. Young people need to know the story of their country; they can profit from an understanding of the rise and decline of other peoples and civilizations; and history's contributions to a general or liberal education as part of the development of cultured individuals should not be discounted. But, while adding to the foregoing knowledge and related skills, history study should also focus on historical investigation, critical thinking, and analytical and decision-making competencies. This portion of school history should lead boys and girls into the search for answers, facts, and veracity.

ORGANIZING HISTORICAL SUBJECT MATTER

Two major concerns face the teacher who is to instruct in the area of history and who desires to lead pupils to employ historical approaches in their own investigations. The first is the curriculum issue—the *what* and *where* elements of the selection and organization of content. The second is the methodological aspect—the *how* element of strategies and techniques.

In some situations teachers have relatively little control over what they will teach. If there is a basic text and a lack of supplemental learning materials, a weak school library, or common grade level or departmental tests, the teacher may be considerably constricted in the subject matter treated. However, state and local curriculum guides have become increasingly more open and suggestive rather than stipulative and directive. Local and individual planning is encouraged. Most teachers are quite free to use textbooks as they see fit. And many schools have a rich variety of materials and media that supports individual teacher independence and creativity.

Before turning our attention to instructional approaches in history, it seems important to emphasize the point that in determining subject matter organization, there is no proved, best way to approach historical content. The traditional, chronological organization, which even Arnold Toynbee called "that one damn thing after another approach," is predominant. And if a teacher's overriding purpose is, unfortunately, to lead pupils to know events in order and cause-and-effect relationships, this time-oriented organization is probably the most efficient. But numerous variations within, or accommodating, a chronological pattern are possible and so, too, are other approaches. As an example, let us consider the different ways that a teacher or school might organize a program in world history. The following columns with their samples of unit subtitles serve to illustrate this important choice:

Chronological organization	Culture/area studies	Conceptual organization	Topical studies
Ancient societies	Western Europe	Progress	Governmental
Greece and Rome	The Middle East	Change	patterns
Middle Ages	Slavonic peoples	Power	Religion through
Byzantine world	Far Eastern	Conflict	the ages
etc.	peoples	etc.	War and peace
	etc.		Education
			etc.

Societies past and present	National emphasis	Themes in human experience	Problem-centered organization
Egyptian life	Rise of Germany	Economics of	(Problems to be
Village in India	Soviet Union	survival	studied can be
Japanese family	Modern China	World of the	preselected and/or
Nigerian tribe	British Empire	family	be the result of
etc.	etc.	Cities through	teacher–pupil
		time	planning.)
		Artistic	
		expression	
		etc.	

Other organizing factors such as the "Basic Human Activities"—transportation, communication, production, use of leisure, etc.—can be suggested in addition to the eight lists above. Various combinations are also possible. The aim is to provide relevant selectivity with adequate breadth and sufficient depth of content.

Similarly, American history can be approached in a variety of ways, and since our school population is normally exposed to United States history three times between fifth and eleventh grades, the problems of organization and emphasis may be greater here than in world history. Again, agreement is called for within districts and/or between high schools and their feeder schools.

41

APPROACHES TO VITALIZE HISTORY INSTRUCTION

Successful approaches to history are limited only by one's imagination. It is a tragedy that some teachers fail to move beyond "2 by 4" instruction—limiting study to the content between the *two* covers of the text and maintaining sterile recitation within the *four* walls of the schoolroom. By contrast, a number of developments are interesting in that they involve historians and teachers in somewhat new or previously overlooked ways to approach, examine, and report history. As a result, descriptive literature and related materials are becoming available that encourage further explorations and extended trials in these directions.

The attractive element in most of these approaches is that they tend to be more motivational than typical read-and-lecture, question-and-answer history lessons. Rather, students tend to find the content relevant because they are involved in discovering, analyzing, interpreting, and writing history—not merely being expected to absorb it.

HISTORY WITH A BROADENED BASE AND ADDED TOOLS

In recent years, historians have frequently been included in teams of researchers on a variety of contemporary studies and projects. The historians have discovered that their interpretations of the backgrounds have often been strengthened by the insights of and the methods applied by social scientists. The results of such joint activity tend to reflect what was recognized by the early progenitors of the idea of the social studies—that no single discipline can adequately explain any social event or development.

History and geography, for example, have always gone hand in hand, and it is difficult to understand how numerous historical happenings can be treated satisfactorily without careful consideration of closely related environmental factors. How else can a history teacher try to explain the life patterns of ancient Egypt, the defeat of the Spanish Armada, the settlement of the Great Plains, or the involvement and entrapment of the United States in Vietnam? While we need to avoid simple geographical determinism, a lack of consideration of geographical conditions in classroom history presentations is all too frequent. Often in history units there is a real lack of helpful map work and little or no use of historical atlases or of related, geographically oriented learning exercises.

In addition to the natural conjunction with geography, history can be further illuminated by contributions from many other disciplines, even those outside of the area of the social sciences. For example, a combination of insights and approaches from art, archeology, and anthropology not only enables pupils to gain an enlarged view of history but also helps promote a recognition of how many aspects of history have to be constructed partially, and sometimes largely, from nonwritten sources. Here observations, tape recordings, and items of realia, for example, may be the only available sources. Numerous photographic collections are available in books, in sets of illustrations, and in slides and filmstrips. Enterprising teachers frequently develop their own sets of slides, and this valuable activity can be extended by encouraging such projects on the part of the students. Pupils also enjoy and are proficient in reproducing artifacts and making models. Classes are sometimes even involved in actual site digs, as well as in the generally less satisfactory artificial or simulated digs. Music teachers may be invited to play and discuss representative songs of different historical eras, and pupils can make class reports using their own record collections. Stamp and coin collections are examples of realia that also directly interest many pupils.

What is important in all such activities is that the pupil is not just copying and the class not just watching. Teachers must develop creative assignments that enable young people to build skills as they inquire and discuss and to draw conclusions about the content with which they have been working.

Another area beyond the social sciences that holds increasing opportunities for those who are historically inclined rises from the realm of computer science. Modern technology now makes it possible to employ mathematics and store vast amounts of information related to historical questions. It will be some years before computers become common in school instruction, but it is possible for pupils who do not have access to computers to employ quantified approaches to historical study. Census facts are among the rich reservoir of information available in such publications as almanacs, and *The Historical Abstract of the United States* holds massive amounts of data suitable for producing a variety of significant charts and graphs as part of the exploration of historical questions. The rows of dry figures on yearly immigration into the United States, for example, become dramatic rising and falling indicators on a visual timeline for the bulletin board to help explain the increases and declines from decade to decade. Public tax and property ownership records can also be revealing sources of information.

History is a most encompassing discipline, and it serves as an excellent medium for handling the interrelationships of human existence. It fulfills a comprehensive "cementing" function, and in schools in the United States we have used history as the major, broad base for social education. Nevertheless, both the microscopic and telescopic aspects of history are greatly enhanced by the funded knowledge and the investigatory tools of other disciplines. To ignore such can be as damaging to the validity of a history teacher's efforts as it can be to the conclusions of historians who do not use such vehicles in carrying on their own research and writing.

HISTORY AS SEEN FROM BELOW

History from the bottom up, as it is now popularly designated, moves attention from the power elites and great individuals to what has happened among the bulk of people, focusing on their concerns, lives, problems, and contributions. Recent years have seen real growth of interest in the history of the common people. Previously some historians have worked in these areas of social and cultural history, but their total effort is a fragment when compared to the attention devoted to political and military history. Our school textbooks have reflected this imbalance. Too frequently, inserted cultural chapters consist of dreary name-and-date entries of famous artists, musicians, and other cultural leaders.

If it is true that the bulk of history available to us represents what has happened in the lives of but 5 percent of humankind (and that primarily of members of the upper echelons of society), redressing of the resulting imbalance is certainly in order. There is also hope here for motivation and a feeling of relevancy on the part of pupils who find in such history numerous reflections of conditions that they to some degree have also experienced. The famous Mr. Dooley, Finley Peter Dunne's sage of old Chicago who entertained so many newspaper readers of an earlier generation, once explained that he knew history wasn't true because it wasn't like what he saw every day from his saloon on Halstead Street. He claimed that history was like a post-mortem, telling what a country died of, but he indicated that he preferred to know how it really lived. He agreed to believe that there was a factual past only when he found a history book showing people making love, quarreling, getting married, and owing the grocery man! Mr. Dooley anticipated the import of approaching history from the bottom up.

Fortunately, more aspects of the lives of the lower or working classes are finding their way into a variety of publications, and teachers should stay alert for such accounts—the letters, diary entries, newspaper reproductions, pictures, and other such resources that can be used to make this element of history come alive. Descriptions of changing rural life, conditions in industrial cities, union growth, labor strife, and changing occupations are all parts of working-class history that are greatly underemphasized in typical texts. Even a picture of a shift of little, wan, coal-blackened boys just up from the mine shafts can truly do as much as a thousand words if, for example, one is concerned with building an understanding of the evils of child labor.

What history as seen from below also provides is the valuable opportunity for youngsters to carry on their own investigations and recreations of the past, including near-current events that are important in their own communities. This is where a growing interest in local history ties in with the history of the common people. This also provides an opportunity to link the school with its enveloping environment as children actually experience the method of history. Such community study also provides for the development of key social studies skills that may be neglected if we focus on studying just national or world history. Local investigations can stretch from field trips of one day or several periods to a nearby industrial plant or a cemetery to extensive, year-long studies of numerous aspects of community life. Some teachers have committees that develop mini-texts or chapters on each aspect of local history being examined by the class, and in some cases these become continuing projects extended by future students over several years.

Teachers interested in local history should also be informed about recent developments in oral history. Significant collections of interviews and accounts by members of the older generation are being gathered at a number of libraries and universities. These tapes can usually be borrowed or copied as fits a school's need. But beyond that, once again, pupils can become engaged in their own oral history programs.

A consideration of the neglected groups in history further leads us to examine the relationships with the growing movements in minority studies and the increased attention to ethnic and women's history. Too often blacks, Latinos, women, and others have not been able to find themselves in history courses. Additionally, some, including the Native Americans and the Chinese Americans, do not appreciate the manner in which their people and heritage are presented in some history books. However, the stream of pamphlets, uni-texts, films, and other resources that have become available promises to remain a significant reservoir upon which teachers can draw to help eliminate neglect of these individuals and groups. The importance of better stressing the roles of underprivileged groups is underscored by Toynbee's concept of "creative minorities." His thesis is that it is the minority groups—not the successful, secure, and satisfied—who tend to push society ahead into change.

An intimate part of history as seen from below is family history.

In the past, family history was devoted largely to accounts of noted families or to geneological studies of ancestors. But that is now changing. What can bring a child closer to history than to have the child ask grandparents about their lives during the Great Depression, about former recreational and leisure-time activities, about changes in foods used and in their preparation, about war-time conditions, etc.? Not only are pupils developing family trees, assembling picture collections, and tracing the migration of their families; also they are following the family's economic progress and various social and cultural changes, including attention to altered family size and individual roles and interests. Comparisons are being drawn and reasons for differences identified, including the external factors that have affected the family and its functions. In all of this, a word of caution: While family history papers are highly motivational and appropriate at both the elementary and the secondary school levels, teachers need to be careful in the guidelines they provide and in the questions they suggest. Potential difficulties and embarrassment can exist for pupils with adverse or nonconventional family backgrounds.

HISTORY AS INQUIRY

In many of the activities suggested in this chapter, students are involved in one form or another of historical inquiry. The continuing message emphasizes that such involvement is motivational and that, through such investigation, pupils will better grasp knowledge they uncover for themselves at the same time that they build important analytical skills that can carry well beyond the history class or lesson.

A number of models have been formulated for teachers to follow in helping pupils develop the requisite competencies. These models reach from the simple, four-step formula Roy Hatch developed for elementary school children—Find the Facts, Filter the Facts, Face the Facts, and Follow the Facts[1]—to far more complex seven- to ten-stage processes that have been outlined for high school students. Essentially, in one form or another, all models include the following four phases:

1. *Clarifying and Identifying a Problem:* In this first phase the topic to be investigated is isolated and agreed upon, the necessary definitions are established, and the subsequent steps to be followed by the class, as well as by subgroups or individual students, are determined. This discussion may or may not lead to some tentative conclusions or hypotheses as to just what, why, or how something happened. These initial formulations can help to

guide the search for data and evidence, but pupils should not become so attached to a guess they have made that they would tend to operate deductively to "prove" what they anticipated.

2. *Searching for Evidence:* As a part of the first phase, the teacher and class have identified some of the resources and materials they will search out and examine. Now, in what is normally the longest phase of this inquiry process, the pupils gather direct evidence; they explore original or primary sources to the extent possible and, typically in school situations, a goodly number of secondary references—those reporting on what someone else experienced. Fortunately, many original descriptions, documents, speeches, diaries, letters, photographs, etc., are now available in special source books, and textbooks are also including increased amounts of source material.

3. *Interpreting and Deciding About the Evidence:* It should be noted that as a class is actively involved in the historical search, clear-cut separations between the phases do not always hold. The human mind and the multiple directions that characterize a search do not normally follow an outlined guide or a model. However, at the beginning of this third phase, all of the available evidence has been gathered and organized to some degree, and further discussion and analysis are now in order. The investigators next consider all of the data in terms of possible bias, degree of objectivity, differing frames of reference, judgments, etc., and are now ready to draw their conclusion or conclusions.

4. *Drawing Historical Conclusions:* The last phase of historical inquiry varies, depending on the type of lesson, the amount of time involved, the depth of the probe, and the purposes of the assignment. In some cases an oral conclusion agreed upon by the class may suffice; in others the pupil or the group may attempt to actually write the best possible reconstruction of the event.

Other questions need to be considered at the end of such searches. For example, if the class has been examining sources and interpretations to decide what really caused the Civil War, the following queries need to be raised: Have we truly isolated the major cause? Was there a single main cause? Can the underlying and the immediate causes be identified and separated? How certain can we be of our conclusions? What helpful prime evidence is not available? Why is it missing? If possible, how could this information be gained? Why have competent historians continued to disagree about these causes?

While there are no "if's" in history, pupils often like to consider alternatives that would have developed if a given key element in a chain of events had been altered. Current future-studies emphases now encourage teachers considering contemporary problems to lead their classes in attempts to develop alternative scenarios of tomorrow. Similar consideration of former events can sharpen the capacity of students to grasp the maze of factors that helped influence those developments and that characterize the complexity of any chain of events, past or present.

Additionally, students should come to understand the typically unique elements of any happening and the danger of attempting to draw any continuing "lesson" or generalization from the incident. Historians rarely generalize, and most would differ with the statement that "history is pretty much the same old things happening to new people." On the other hand, many aspects of human nature seem to have remained very constant over time, and long-lived societies tend to ingrain similar cultural attitudes and reactions. Environmental factors such as weather patterns throughout the globe also tend to remain constant with but minimal fluctuations. Thus, within limits it may be possible to go beyond the fact finding, the skill and concept building, and the disparate conclusions in an attempt to draw tentative generalizations about humankind and their affairs, especially if similar instances have occurred a number of times in the past in different places and eras.

MOTIVATIONS IN HISTORY STUDY

Motivation has been called the-half-of-learning and with the modern appeals outside of the classroom—especially in the realm of media —teachers face a continuing challenge; for most pupils it is difficult to make the history lesson as exciting as Buck Rogers. Nevertheless, creative and colorful teachers find intriguing ways to make the schoolroom inviting and the learning of history enjoyable and rewarding.

Teachers need to share approaches and keep alert for what can be borrowed. There is a need to read professional magazines such as *The History Teacher* and *Social Education,* to examine the academic journals to keep up with new findings and new interpretations, to use professional leave days to visit outstanding programs and teachers, to keep a file of successful activities and valuable resources, to use the materials available in local curriculum or teacher centers, and to be well informed and alert on contemporary affairs. Above all, there is a need to find the means to communicate with other teachers handling the same subject.

Such a regimen will help extensively in keeping one well informed, lively, and interesting.

REFERENCE

1. Hatch, Roy W. "The Project-Problem as a Method for Teaching History." *The Historical Outlook,* June 1920. pp. 237–240.

Additional Readings

Alder, Douglas D., and Linden, Glenn M., editors. *Teaching World History.* Boulder, Colo.: Social Science Education Consortium, 1977.

Botein, Stephen, and others, editors. *Experiments in History Teaching.* Cambridge, Mass.: Harvard–Danforth Center for Teaching and Learning, 1977.

Cartwright, William H., and Watson, Richard L., Jr., editors. *Interpreting and Teaching American History.* Thirty-First Yearbook of the National Council for the Social Studies. Washington, D.C.: the Council, 1961.

Commager, Henry Steele. *The Nature and The Study of History.* Columbus, Ohio: Charles E. Merrill, 1965.

Daniels, Robert V. *Studying History: How and Why.* (Englewood Cliffs, N.J.: Prentice-Hall, 1966.

Dickinson, A.K., and Lee, P.J., editors. *History Teaching and Historical Understanding.* London: Heinemann, 1978.

Gawronski,Donald V.*History: Meaning and Method.* Glenview, Ill.: Scott, Foresman, 1969.

Gustavson, Carl. *A Preface to History.* New York: McGraw-Hill, 1955.

Johnson, Henry. *Teaching of History in Elementary and Secondary Schools.* New York: Macmillan, 1940.

Kownslar, Allan O., editor. *Teaching American History: The Quest for Relevancy.* Forty-Fourth Yearbook of the National Council for the Social Studies. Washington, D.C.: the Council, 1974.

————. *Teaching About Social Issues in American History.* Boulder, Colo.: Social Science Education Consortium, 1978.

Leinwand, Gerald. *Teaching of World History.* Bulletin No. 54. Washington, D.C.: National Council for the Social Studies, 1978.

Levy, Tedd, and Krasnow, Donna Collins. *A Guidebook for Teaching United States History: Earliest Times to the Civil War* and *Mid-Nineteenth Century to the Present.* Boston: Longwood Div., Allyn and Bacon, 1979. 2 vols.

Linden, Glenn M., and Downey, Matthew T., editors. *Teaching American History: Structured Inquiry Approaches.* Boulder, Colo.: Social Science Education Consortium, 1975.

Nevins, Allan. *Gateway to History.* Boston: D.C. Heath, 1962.

Reel, Valleda J. *1818 Activities for Teaching World History Classes.* Portland, Maine: J. Weston Walch, 1974.

Stephens, Lester D. *Probing the Past.* Boston: Allyn and Bacon, 1975.

Thorton, Willis. *Fable, Fact and History.* Philadelphia: Chilton, 1959.

Thursfield, Richard E., editor. *The Study and Teaching of American History.* Seventeenth Yearbook of the National Council for the Social Studies. Washington, D.C.: the Council, 1946.

Ward, Paul L. *A Style of History for Beginners.* Pub. No. 22. Washington, D.C.: American Historical Association, Service Center for Teachers of History, 1959.

West, Edith, editor. *Improving the Teaching of World History.* Twentieth Yearbook of the National Council for the Social Studies. Washington, D.C.: the Council, 1949.

To say that "Houston is the fifth largest city in the United States" may be interesting. It is not, however, strictly a geographic fact. To state that "Houston, the fifth largest city in the United States, is the most rapidly growing metropolitan area in the Sun Belt region" does add a locational element. The Sun Belt, obviously, lacks the locational precision of latitude and longitude, but it does provide spatial clues. The observor of this fact will know that Houston is located in that southern tier of states that has come to be designated the Sun Belt. Data of a locational nature, then, have now been provided, turning our statement into a geographic fact.

The number of geographic facts that might be assembled for the purpose of curriculum building is virtually interminable. Facts by themselves, however, are simply facts.

Granted, there are those persons who delight in the accumulation of a vast array of such facts, which on the surface appear to be monuments of geographic wisdom. Some geographers delight in wowing their audiences—students or colleagues—by rattling off such unassorted miscellanea as the 1920 population of Pocatello and the number of tons of copper mined at Bingham Canyon since the first shovel bit into ore-laden Utah soil.

Such facts, of course, are often important building blocks in generating geographic concepts. By themselves, however, they provide little that is challenging to the learner. Indeed, it has been said, quite wisely, that one can collect facts without thinking, but that one cannot think without having collected facts. That is, precisely, the purpose of geographic facts. They lead the learner directly to one of four fundamental concepts in geography: *spatial distribution, areal association, spatial interaction,* and *regionalization.* These concepts are so important in understanding the role of geography in the social studies for the 1980's that they warrant our close examination.

Spatial Distribution

A geographic fact dealing with a specific phenomenon within a given piece of space (or place) is a *spatial distribution.* What kinds of phenomena and what sorts of space?

We might, for example, be interested in the location of school-age children in a given county. The phenomenon is the location (or distribution) of school-age children. The place is the given county. We could refine this spatial distribution in a variety of ways—by age or grade grouping, by sex, by race, by I.Q., by socioeconomic family background, or by virtually any other variable with which one might wish to deal.

The place, however, is fixed: It is limited to the boundaries of the county under investigation. Place, then, is essential if we are to retain a geographic focus.

The kinds of spatial distributions that interest geographers are as varied as their areas of specialization. Spatial distributions may, for example, include diverse physical phenomena such as climate, soils, landforms, and vegetation; economic phenomena such as manufacturing, transportation, and resources; and cultural phenomena such as languages, religions, and house-types. The places may range in scale from the area of a single farm to that of the entire surface of the earth.

Areal Association

Our second basic concept involves two or more spatial distributions. In other words, the concept of *areal association* is built upon the concept of a close correspondence of two spatial distributions in the same place, which, in turn, is a concept built on geographic fact. Principally areal association involves the spatial distribution of one phenomenon that is affected by or dependent on the spatial distribution of another phenomenon.

The possible combinations are numerous, indeed. Within the boundaries of a given metropolitan area, for example, the spatial distribution of freeways and the spatial distribution of shopping centers clearly demonstrate an areal association. The spatial distribution of corn production within counties in a given midwestern state and the spatial distribution of swine production in the same state demonstrate to an amazing degree areal association: Counties in which large quantities of corn are grown almost invariably have large numbers of swine. In this case, clearly, one distribution ties directly to the other.

Spatial Interaction

In focusing on the concept of areal association, only one place, or area, is involved. In dealing with the concept of spatial interaction, geographers shift their locational attention to two places and examine the ties or linkages between them.

The concept of spatial interaction is fundamental to modern geography because modern geography is particularly concerned with the relationships and interactions between phenomena over the surface of the earth. These relationships and interactions imply the flow of goods, the movement of people, and even the dissemination of ideas. Regardless of whether we are studying the volume of the flow of goods, the number of people who move, or the speed with which new ideas are disseminated, we are focusing specifically on spatial interaction.

It is not essential to the concept of spatial interaction, however, that vast, world-scale distances be involved. We could focus on several locations within an urban area. We might, for example, focus on specific residential neighborhoods and the places where the residents of these areas work. This journey-to-work problem involves two specific pieces of space—residence space and work space. These two separate pieces of space have connections or spatial interaction. In other words, people are interacting through space. Thus, the very term *spatial interaction* is descriptive of the idea to which it is attached.

The amount of spatial interaction that can occur between phenomena represented by two individual geographic facts can be affected by a host of factors, three of which are absolutely basic to all spatial interaction models: complementarity, separation, and transferability.

Complementarity refers to the relationship that exists between phenomena that are part of a process or that provide a way of producing something or of accomplishing a particular result. In other words, there must be a surplus (supply) of something in one place and a shortage (demand) in another place.

There is a surplus of oil in the Persian (Arabian) Gulf area. There is a demand for it in the United States. Despite the distance and the cost, complementarity exists and lines of flow are established.

Separation is implicit in the concept of spatial interaction—two separate pieces of space are involved. The phenomena involved do not occupy the same piece of space as they do in areal association.

Typically we think of separation, or the distance between phenomena, in terms of miles or kilometers. For many geographic problems that focus on spatial interaction, however, economic distance is of far greater significance. There are two ways of measuring economic distance—in dollar costs and in time costs. Where complements are part of an economic process, as in the assembling of iron, coal, and limestone in the manufacture of steel, the measurement of separation in terms of either dollars or time may have much greater meaning than separation in terms of miles.

Transferability, the third factor necessary to spatial interaction, refers to the conditions of movement. Thus, transferability is a function of distance measured in cost or time terms, as well as a function of the specific nature of the product. Continuing improvement in transportation and communication permits inexpensive as well as rapid transfer of goods that was almost impossible a century ago. Think, for example, of the rapid transfer, at relatively low cost, of fresh vegetables in the winter from south Florida to markets in the Northeast.

Regionalization

In listing and discussing the four concepts basic to geography for the 1980's, it is appropriate that we focus on the region after having first dealt with the concepts of spatial distribution, areal association, and spatial interaction. The reason is simple: The regional concept is related to all three of the others. The concept of the region can, indeed, be derived from any one of the other concepts. We can find regions that are derived from spatial distributions, from areal associations, and from spatial interactions. First, however, let us examine the meaning of the term *region*.

Geographic literature is replete with scholarly efforts to carefully define a region. Precise definitions, however, are likely to be of less importance to the user of this book than are the ideas that lie behind the definitions.

Essential to the region, as in all geographic study, is the idea of *place*. It is place that is at the heart of all work in geography. It matters little whether the geographer is a fourth-grade student who is coming to grips with the diversity of the planet Earth for the first time or a world-renowned research geographer who is pushing back the frontiers of learning.

Geography, in its regional mode, focuses on questions that explore the patterns of those physical and cultural phenomena that give places their special character. Regional analysis deals with questions such as how and why places, or regions, differ.

Traditionally, geographers have identified several types of regions, the most common of which are known as *homogeneous regions* and *functional regions*. They are not literally mutually exclusive, but, nonetheless, they do have their individual goals and methods of analysis.

In the past, homogeneous regions have been used most often for social studies curriculum development. A homogeneous region, as its name implies, is determined on the basis of one or more independent qualities of likeness, or homogeneity. Most common, for school purposes, have been regions that possess political homogeneity—the United States, France, Tanzania, etc. Political regions, however, are but one type among many homogeneous regions. Soil regions, vegetation regions, and a Cotton Belt region are all illustrations.

In recent years, and particularly as we consider the application of geography in the 1980's, geographers have given increased attention to functional regions. Here they employ their spatial knowledge in understanding how a region functions as a unity rather than by asking simply what gives character to the place. The focus in still on place, or, "Where?" but a shift is made from, "What?" to, "How?" In functional regions, geographers seek out the connections, linkages, and relationships among phenomena within a region. Do you see, therefore, the significance of the concept of areal association in such studies?

Political units are often too diverse to make meaningful functional regions. Linkages across political lines may be more important than internal linkages. Trade areas, transportation networks, and river basins may be better analyzed. In such instances the concept of spatial interaction becomes operational in the regional concept. In political regions, boundaries must be accepted as givens. Often, however, the functions or processes that are studied in functional regions tell us where the boundaries should be. In other words, the functions themselves determine their own regions.

What about the concept of spatial distribution and the region? It may, indeed, be the most commonly used determinant of a region. We might draw a map in which we would include, on a world scale, all of the areas on earth in which spring wheat is the dominant crop. Our map would include large areas of the Dakotas, Montana, and Minnesota, as well as portions of the prairie provinces of Canada. Another large area would appear in the Soviet Union. Our map has provided us with a homogeneous region: a world-scale map of the earth's spring wheat region.

TIES TO THE HABITAT

We began this chapter by referring to the linkages that exist between geography and history. In thinking of the social studies for the 1980's we would ignore these very real ties at our peril. Geography fills a unique spatial role in this accord.

Geography's linkages are not alone to history and the social sciences, however. Indeed, geography, perhaps more than any other discipline, forms bridges between the natural and the social sciences. By its very nature, geography has one foot in the natural sciences through its concerns with the distributions, associations, and interactions among climate, soil, vegetation, and landforms. At the same time, geography is a people-based discipline, interested in the distributions, associations, and interactions among people and their works over the surface of the earth.

In the past two decades perhaps nothing has swept through the conscience of the western world as has concern over the seemingly imminent destruction of our environment. Wave after wave of anger, as well as anxiety, over air and water pollution has engulfed many of the urban–industrial societies of this planet.

Death from toxic smog has occurred in several communities in such widely separated areas as the United States, Belgium, and England. Radioactive fallout, imperiling people and beasts alike, has proved to be a real danger to life. Streams foam with detergents. Rivers have become sewers, and some even fire hazards. Lakes have been declared "dead." Oil spills have threatened sensitive shoreline habitats on a worldwide scale.

As we move through the 1980's, *ecology* is a household word and the "quality of the environment" a universal slogan. Scarcely a social studies program survived the 1970's that did not state that ecology (in spite of its natural science base) was one of the integrated social science disciplines in the program. Photographs of smoke-spewing factories, smoldering slag heaps, and oil-covered birds are found in virtually every successful textbook series. Unhappily, however, much of the content has been superficial and emotion-charged, and has contributed little toward helping young people understand the problems, let alone develop the skills to tackle the solutions.

Geography, certainly, is not a magical discipline. Yet it can be of great help in curriculum-building processes that face the difficulties of including meaningful ecological content in the social studies. This is a topic that will be much with us in the 1980's as smog continues to increase in urban–industrial areas, as carbon dioxide in our atmosphere continues to build, and as energy shortages threaten our very way of life.

The social sciences tend to focus on people as social, economic, and political beings, and to pay little attention to the interactions among people and their habitat. Only two sciences, really, are equipped to deal with the impact of people on their habitat—ecology and geography. Most ecologists, however, tend to focus on the purity of a biological habitat—the tropical rain forest, the coral reef—while geographers have always been more concerned with ecosystems as modified by people.

Geographers abandoned environmentalism as a useful concept half a century ago. It is not nature that shapes the behavior of people; rather, the interactions of people and their habitat are functions of the attitudes, objectives, and technologies of people themselves. People are chosers. People make the decisions as to the ways in which they will bring the resources of any habitat into productive use. And it is geography that focuses on this interaction between people and habitat.

CONCLUSION

What about geography and the social studies for the 1980's? Geography can and must play a major role in the social studies for this decade.

Our planet is tiny and fragile amidst the expanse of space. It is less than 25,000 miles in diameter at the equator. Who of us has not owned an automobile that has gone many times that distance? Yet, by the end of the decade, 5 billion of us will be sharing not only this limited planet but also the resources that it provides. Geography has so much to offer to learners as they come to grips with the realities of place and people. The "place name" geography of the past, the "strange lands and funny people" stereotypical geography of the past, however, will not help.

This chapter has attempted to stake out some conceptual guidelines for the integration of geography within the social studies. It is an eclectic subject, drawing its data from both the social and the natural sciences. Its uniqueness lies in its viewpoint—spatial. As occupants of this tiny piece of firmament, traveling endlessly through the vastness of our universe on our annual trip around the sun, surely a spatial view is essential for our survival and for the survival of our children.

REFERENCE

1. Heylyn, Peter. *Microcosmos, A Little Description of the Great World.* Fifth edition. Oxford: William Turner and Robert Allot, 1631. p. 16.

CHAPTER 6

Cultural Pluralism and the Social Studies

John Jarolimek

Cultural pluralism refers to the diversity in patterns of living and of social heritages of people in American society. This chapter discusses some of the implications of such diversity for the social studies curriculum. The subject is highly susceptible to subjectivity and emotionalism. It is loaded with issues that do not lend themselves to reasoned resolution on the basis of empirical data and expertise. For the past two decades, when this topic has been discussed, there has been a consistent tendency to confuse realities with myths, problems with solutions, and intimidating rhetoric with competent authority. Thus, in some instances, educational policy decisions based on the ideology of pluralism have been made without the benefit of objective analysis. Even more rarely have they been based on research that would speak to their long-term social consequences. Indeed, many such policy decisions have been formulated for political, rather than educational, reasons.

DEVELOPING A NATIONAL IDENTITY

There is good reason to believe that pluralism is now generally accepted as a social reality by the educational leadership in this country. Pluralism in the sense of the multicultural, multiethnic, and multiracial legacies of Americans is simply not an arguable issue. From the earliest invasion by Europeans, the geographic area now defined as the United States has had these "multi" characteristics. By the time of the American Revolution, the Colonies were already populated by a heterogeneous mixture of people from a wide variety of cultures, ethnic groups, and racial backgrounds. Moreover, the Spanish had already penetrated what was later to become the United States' Southwest and had established mission settlements there. At the same time, the French influence was apparent in the Great Lakes and the Ohio–Mississippi Valley regions. Nor should it be forgotten that the entire area was inhabited by various tribes of native people.

Until recently, however, the tendency in social and political education has been to ignore or to denigrate the contributions of heritages other than English—or "Anglo." It was assumed that those who immigrated from non-Anglo homelands would forsake their ancestral roots and become Americans by embracing the values, norms, mores, and lifeways of the dominant, mainstream culture. This meant that they had to learn the American variant of the English language, send their children to school, get their citizenship "papers," serve in the armed forces, and so on. They were simply expected to leave Old World ways behind. In recent years some authors have made a big issue of the notion that this acculturation process stripped the immigrants of their ethnic identity and that those immigrants perceived this as a tragic personal loss. The fact is that while many, perhaps most, had some feelings of nostalgia for their former homelands and desperately missed the loved ones whom they left behind, they were proud, pleased, and, in most cases, anxious to become Americanized.

Those who have been critical of this country's policies in promoting its melting pot ideology have claimed that "to Americanize meant to Anglicize." This is probably an accurate assertion. After all, the Founding Fathers of this nation were either Englishmen themselves or English in their outlook and value orientation. English customs prevailed in trade and industry. The dominant language was English, as was the legal system; many of our laws are derived from English common law. Thus, although the individuals who populated the Colonies were products of many different cultures, the colonies were, in fact, English in terms of the values, traditions, and lifeways that dominated day-to-day social and commercial intercourse. In time, these dominant English influences were diluted and then nearly lost altogether with the infusion of people from other cultures with other orientations. Nevertheless, many of them persist even today.

Throughout the nineteenth century, the United States was developing a unique national identity. Thus, when this country was receiving immigrants by the millions, particularly between 1890 and 1910, the melting pot metaphor was not an altogether inappropriate one to symbolize the process of acculturation of immigrant people. Can you imagine the chaos and conflict that would have resulted if each immigrant group had been encouraged to segregate itself according to its ethnic identity? Keeping in mind that between 1824 and 1924 some 36 million people immigrated to this country—the largest movement of people in human history—the fact that the United States was able to absorb these people without a major civil uprising has to be considered one of the most remarkable social achievements of all time.

Today it is apparent that there are many things wrong with the melting pot idea. But at the turn of the century when each year the country was receiving hundreds of thousands of non-English-speaking immigrants from eastern and southern Europe, the challenge of getting these people into the mainstream culture as quickly and as painlessly as possible was worrisome to the leaders of the time. Considering that as late as 1920, 40 percent of the nation was still of foreign stock— meaning that they were immigrants or children of immigrant parents— it is remarkable that the process worked as well as it did.

THE RISE OF PLURALISM

The ascendancy of pluralism is often associated with the civil rights activism of the early 1960's. While the civil rights movement was, undoubtedly, partially responsible for the revitalization of interest in ethnic identity, it is far from an adequate explanation for the rise of pluralism in American life. Pluralism can exist only when people are able to choose how they are to live. This means that the economy must be competitive to the extent that it can provide people with choices, that the governmental structure must permit diversity, that the technology must be advanced enough to create alternatives from which to choose, and, most importantly, that individuals must be psychologically secure enough to make choices. Henry Ford I who mass-produced the Model T is often quoted as having said that a buyer could have the car in any color as long as it was black! All of the early Model T Fords had four-cylinder engines, with a magneto for electrical energy, rear-wheel mechanical brakes, and a planetary transmission. Today's car buyer has hundreds, perhaps even thousands, of options if one takes into account all of the permutations possible regarding makes, models, engines, colors, upholstery, accessories, and so on. The same wide range of choice exists in almost all facets of modern life. Small villages of five or six hundred persons may have as many as a dozen churches. In the health care field there are medical doctors, chiropractors, osteopaths, naturopaths, herb doctors, and faith healers to accommodate individual needs and persuasions. Individuals have even been creative in designing alternatives to the conventional husband–wife marriage. One would be hard put to think of anything that people do in this society in which they do not have a choice.

The term *cultural pluralism* was first used by Horace M. Kallen in 1924,[1] but it only recently has come into widespread use. It is not altogether appropriate to limit the meaning of cultural pluralism to ethnic diversity because, as we have seen from the foregoing paragraph, cultural pluralism can take many forms. Because we have a pluralistic orientation to almost everything associated with our life-style, there is a greater readiness to accept the idea of diversity of ethnic heritages. In other words, it is now "OK" to be of Polish, Indian, Black, Asian, Irish, or Italian extraction, whereas a generation ago such identity would have carried a stigma. There is no question that this society has made great strides in building such attitudes of acceptance in recent years. Of course, the job is not yet completed, and we still have a way to go.

Today the nation does not face the same concerns and problems that it faced at the turn of the century. The number of immigrants it receives, even including those from Southeast Asia, is miniscule when compared with the influx of people between 1890 and 1910. Furthermore, many of the immigrants who have entered the United States in recent years have been educated persons with well-developed skills, often with professional training. Because these people can easily be absorbed into the population, they pose no threat to the stability or security of the nation. Many of the descendants of the poor and illiterate immigrants of the earlier period, whether they came from Europe, Africa, Asia, or Latin America, are now thoroughly assimilated into mainstream American life. In other words, this may be the first generation of Americans that is psychologically secure enough to deal with the reality of pluralism that has resulted from a multiethnic heritage. The interest in and the greater acceptance of ethnic diversity, then, can be interpreted as an extension of widespread cultural pluralism.

Although the terms *multicultural* and *bicultural* are often loosely applied to the diversity of ethnic heritages, it must be understood that very few Americans are brought up in a culture that stands wholly apart from the mainstream culture. The international districts of cities—the Chinatowns, the Little Mexicos, the Harlems, and so on—are not totally separate cultures. They are, at best, subcultures, containing much from the mainstream, with variations added as a result of a particular ethnic experience or heritage. It is only when we encounter groups in remote areas, or those who have otherwise isolated themselves from the rest of society, that we get close to what might be considered another culture, as, for example, certain Indian and Eskimo groups or such religious groups as the Hutterites and Mennonites. But even in those cases, it is debatable whether they are second cultures or simply subcultures, especially when we see snowmobiles or pick-up trucks parked in their yards or television antennas emerging from the roofs of their dwellings. A recent newspaper photograph showed a barefoot, teen-aged Mennonite girl holding what appeared to be an animated conversation in a streetside telephone booth because phones are not allowed in Mennonite homes. Next to the telephone booth, her horse, hitched to a buggy, waited patiently! This young woman is dealing with a personal reality that many Americans have had to face—that of adapting their lives to the demands of the mainstream culture without at the same time totally alienating themselves from the culture of their forebearers.

In social studies education, cultural pluralism should be taught as a broad concept having to do with the many variations and options in life-style that people have available to them. This is, of course, a form of human relations education. Helping learners develop the maturity to make their own life choices and, at the same time, to respect the right of others to make different choices is one of the great challenges to social studies teachers.

MULTIETHNIC EDUCATION IN THE SOCIAL STUDIES

An ethnic group is an aggregate of individuals who have a shared history, speak a common language, hold similar religious beliefs, observe common traditions, have a sense of nationality, have their own folklore, and develop what some authors have referred to as a sense of "peoplehood." The term *ethnicity* has to do with the unique characteristics one has developed as a consequence of one's ethnic identity. It is important to understand that ethnic behavior or ethnicity is learned; it is not transmitted genetically. Physical qualities—i.e., racial identity—on the other hand, *are* genetically transmitted from parents to children and may or may not be associated with ethnic identity. For example, there are many persons in the United States who have the physical characteristics of Asians, Africans, American Indians, or Latinos, but who have no psychological or social attachments whatever to those particular ethnic groups. Yet, if those same individuals had been brought up in their ancestral cultures, their physical appearance would be regarded as an intrinsic part of their ethnic identity.

Most nations of the world have a few ethnic minority populations —for example, the Laplanders in northern Norway, the Basques in northern Spain, and the Palestinians in Israel—but for the most part, the nations remain predominantly of a single ethnic composition. The situation in the United States is clearly different. Here many ethnic groups have been socialized into the mainstream culture; yet remnants of their ethnic origins often persist—in some cases, very strongly and for several generations. In other words, people of different ethnic origins in the United States may have been acculturated, but only in varying degrees have they been assimilated—i.e., rendered indistinguishable from mainstream America.

This country is unique among the nations of the world in that its citizens can trace their ancestral roots to all of the world's many cultures. We are, therefore, *multiethnic* in our origins, and the evidence of our multiethnic legacy is all around us. The people of the United States truly represent a confluence of world cultures. Some individuals have stronger ethnic attachments than do others, and some, rejecting the idea of ethnic identity altogether, simply say they are "American." But a surprisingly high percentage of Americans does claim some ethnic identity. An individual who may be a mixture of a half-dozen or more ethnic or national groups will often select one and embrace it as his or her ethnic group—"I'm Irish," "I'm Indian," "I'm Polish," and so on. The ethnic group with which he or she identifies may not even be the dominant one in his or her background.

Many aspects of our multiethnic heritage, along with contemporary cultural pluralism, have become institutionalized in social studies programs in recent years. These emphases are reflected in modern textbooks and curriculum documents. They have become an accepted part of the mainstream social studies program in many schools. Much remains to be done, however, if the school program is to play a significant role in combatting racism, ethnocentrism, and social injustice stemming from ethnic identity. The following recommendations suggest directions in which multiethnic education could profitably move:

1. American history, as taught in elementary and secondary schools, should focus on immigration history in order to portray more adequately the contributions of many world cultures to the development of the American nationality.

2. A variety of educational experiences should be provided to help young people develop a sensitivity to ethnic diversity and learn to respect differences that are a result of ethnic heritage.

3. Young people should have opportunities to learn something about their personal ethnic heritage, if they choose to do so. However, the heavily affective and emotional aspects of ethnic identity should be discouraged—particularly if such an emphasis results in the ethnic issue's becoming a weapon of social and political power. By promoting exaggerated ethnic pride, the school simply encourages attitudes of ethnocentrism that can result in unwholesome intergroup relations.

4. The multiethnic emphasis should be integrated into the program at all grade levels, K–12, and should not be reserved simply for a unit or topic to be studied outside the mainstream social studies curriculum.

5. The positive values of ethnic diversity should be stressed. Life is richer and more interesting, and it provides many more opportunities for choice because of the ethnic variety of our people. It is not only the native Hawaiian people who enjoy a luau. And who would say that a trip to San Francisco would be complete without a visit to Chinatown? Or to New Orleans without enjoying the fine cuisine of the French Quarter and the jazz music of Preservation Hall? Of course, cross-cultural understanding involves more than tasting foods and dressing in a native costume on an ethnic holiday. The essential point is this: The advantage of an ethnically diverse heritage is that anyone and everyone can participate in and benefit from whatever each group has to offer. Ethnic diversity need not be a divisive force in society; indeed, it can be a means of promoting social cohesiveness.

It should be said, finally, that the social studies program of our public schools has a first responsibility to focus on those overarching common values such as freedom, equality, justice, humanity, self-government, and human dignity that for over two hundred years have held us together as "one Nation . . . indivisible." The engendering of ethnic attachments and ethnic pride in the young and the emphasis on pluralism and diversity cannot be permitted to develop uncontrollably without creating unwanted social side effects. Social studies education in the years ahead will need to achieve a balance in emphasis of the kind embodied in the following statement made by President Carter in his nomination acceptance address in 1976:

We can have an America that encourages and takes pride in our ethnic diversity, our religious diversity, our cultural diversity, knowing that out of this pluralistic heritage has come the strength and vitality and creativity that has made America great and will keep us great.

REFERENCE

1. Kallen, Horace M. *Culture and Democracy in the United States.* New York: Boni and Liveright, 1924.

CHAPTER 7

Social Studies for an Urbanized World

Carole L. Hahn

A recent National Science Foundation survey of social studies in the United States reported that during the period from 1955 to 1975 elementary school textbooks contained increasingly fewer examples of rural life and increasingly more urban material.[1] That shift reflects a population change not only in the United States but also in the rest of the world.

Seventy-five percent of the people in the United States now live in urban areas—cities and their outward spreading suburbs. The urbanization of entire nations, like the United States, is a relatively new phenomenon, though cities are not new. The Industrial Revolution caused the urban revolution—first in England, then in the rest of Europe, the United States, Japan, and other industrialized nations. Currently, a fantastic growth of cities is occurring in Latin America, Asia, and Africa. Half of the world's people will be living in cities by 1990.

"Whether we live in the central city, in the suburbs, or in rural America, urbanism is a part of all of our lives," emphasizes Richard Wisniewski, editor of the 1972 National Council for the Social Studies Yearbook, *Teaching About Life in the City.*[2] That point was brought home to us when newspaper editorials across the country debated whether taxpayers' money should be used to "bail out" New York City from bankruptcy. The nightly television situation comedies, advertising, and news from cities across the globe have urbanized us all. Both the problems and the possibilities of the cities belong to each of us. Students must learn that alternative futures are possible for an urbanized world and that the decisions they make will contribute to determining which alternative becomes the reality.

What distinguishes an urbanized world from a formerly rural one, and what are the implications of that shift for social studies education? How can we help students to understand urban life and to act effectively in an urbanized global culture? Those are the questions that this chapter will address.

Most importantly, urban life everywhere is characterized by a high degree of interdependence. Not only must one satisfy basic needs by purchasing goods and services in the marketplace with money received for one's specialized work, but also a disruption in any part of the urban area causes disruption in one's own life. Strikes by teachers or garbage workers, boycotts by truck drivers, layoffs at plants, and dense fog at an airport are painful directly for some people and indirectly for almost everyone else in the area if the disaster lasts for an extended period of time. Initial inconveniences, restricted services, and lost income develop into economic depressions, health hazards, and political crises. Urban interdependence is of an impersonal nature, which is distinguished from rural independence or interaction with known individuals.

Urban life is characterized by high mobility and decreased family ties, with an increased tendency to belong to many different groups. Social problems are most acute in urban areas. Cities all over the world often have the highest rates of unemployment, shortages of adequate housing, decaying buildings, congested traffic, high crime rates, crowded courts and prisons, insufficient health care, and schools characterized by violence and poor learning environments. In cities in the United States, these problems are compounded by the fact that the tax base to pay for the needed services is diminishing. Many urban dwellers feel helpless against overwhelming conditions and alienated from the political decision makers.

Urbanization also generates some of the most positive features of modern life. New buildings reflecting the most recent advances in technology stand next to old buildings that symbolize the cultural heritage. Rich and poor people of all ages represent heterogeneous populations. The close proximity of ethnic groups in cities provides the opportunity to learn from a variety of ethnic restaurants, festivals, churches, art exhibits, stores, publications, and ceremonies. It is in cities that one finds museums, professional sports, centers for the arts, and a tremendous variety of goods and services. And cities offer the great diversity of jobs that draws new urban dwellers from the farms.

Both the problems and the possibilities of the world's cities demand that students develop skill in decision making and in effective social participation. Because the fate of an urbanized world rests with all of our citizens, social studies programs must help students to reflect upon urban issues. And because most students will at some time live in urban areas, we must prepare them to live there in a satisfying way. The elements of an adequate social studies program for an urbanized world are suggested by the four dimensions of the *Curriculum Guidelines* of the National Council for the Social Studies (NCSS).[3]

In the *knowledge dimension,* students must learn facts, concepts, and generalizations that will help them to comprehend society and to take part in it successfully. Studies of urban living will combine knowledge from the arts, law, philosophy, the communication media, history, and the social sciences. Examples of some social science concepts that are useful to understanding urbanization are:

History: conflict, social change
Sociology: values, status, institutions
Anthropology: culture, tradition, acculturation, ethnic group
Geography: cultural diffusion, spatial interaction, land-use patterns
Political science: power, government, political efficacy
Economics: division of labor, interdependence, circular flow of income

Generalizations from the social sciences also can be developed or tested by students as they study urbanization in different places during different time periods. The following examples were selected from *Teaching Strategies for the Social Studies* by James A. Banks:[4]

History (from studies of cities in the past). A historian's view of the past is influenced by the availability of evidence, his or her personal biases and purposes for writing, and the society and times in which he or she lives and works.

Sociology (from studies of life in cities in different parts of the world today). Groups are often the victims of discrimination and prejudice because of age, sex, race, religious or cultural differences.

Anthropology (also from studies of life in cities in different parts of the world today). All societies have a set of traditions that help maintain group solidarity and identity.

Geography (from studies of cities over several time periods—e.g. Chicago, London, Tokyo, Cairo, New Delhi). The sequence of activities and culture patterns is related to geographic location and accessibility, and to the particular time in which human beings live.

Political science (from newspaper articles about students' own city and guest speakers). Organized interest groups attempt to influence the making of public policy when they believe that such policy will affect their goals.

Economics (from studies of United States cities over the past 50 years). Government has become increasingly a participant in the market economy. It is a competitor and also a creator of economic opportunities.

Many social scientists specialize in urban issues. Professors from nearby universities ought to be invited to speak to students about the work of urban geographers, urban anthropologists, and urban sociologists, and about the potential careers in their applied fields.

The second dimension of the social studies curriculum is *abilities*— the bond between knowledge and decision making. Included in abilities are data processing and intellectual and human relations competencies. To understand and to function in the urbanized world, citizens must be able to read critically, write clearly, and speak persuasively. They must be able to listen carefully, interpret charts and graphs appropriately, and read maps accurately. Social studies classes provide excellent opportunities for the development of these abilities. They also provide opportunities to develop such social skills as being sensitive to others, communicating, coping with frustration or disappointment, dealing with conflict and authority, leading and following others, and making contributions to group efforts. And, finally, social studies must develop thinking skills. To solve the problems of the urbanized world, citizens must be able to analyze, synthesize, and evaluate. They must be able to apply relevant information to questions and to critically reflect upon data before drawing conclusions.

As the NCSS *Curriculum Guidelines* note, abilities are not developed as a result of accumulating information, but rather they are acquired through constant practice. The activities listed below are sample ideas for providing that practice.

Elementary School

1. Listen to stories about children in cities in different parts of the world.

2. Write a song, a poem, or a story about a child in a city.

3. Interview family members to find out how many cities they have lived in or visited.

71

4. Make a class chart about the cities that students have lived in or visited.

5. Examine photographs from many modern cities. List all the kinds of transportation you see.

6. Compare and contrast community helpers in cities around the world.

7. Using photographs from cities around the world, group together pictures of housing that seem similar. Explain how the pictures in one pile are alike and how they are different from the pictures in other piles.

8. Make a collection of tools used by different workers. Handle the tools and discuss how they are used. Draw a picture of a worker using each tool on the job in the city.

Middle School

1. Interview old people about how their lives changed when they moved to the city.

2. Interview people who have lived in cities outside of the United States, asking them how living in other cities is similar to and different from where they live now.

3. Using several different sources, try to answer the following question: What were the causes of population growth at different periods for cities in your state? Before searching for information, record a hypothesis, and think of several places where you might get information. As you search, notice points of agreement and disagreement in your sources. (This can be done using only books in the school library, but individuals or groups could also visit a local museum or historical society, or talk with a state history professor or public relations personnel in large industries.)

4. Construct models of cities of the past.

5. Write a newspaper for a city of the past. Include sports, entertainment, and weather as well as news, editorials, advertising, and letters to the editor.

6. Make a collection of news clippings that shows how people in your community are connected to people in cities outside of the United States. At the end of a month write several paragraphs to summarize your findings.

7. Using city maps (obtained from travel clubs, tourist bureaus, embassies, etc.) for different cities in the world, practice planning a route from one place to another.

8. Conduct a social scientific inquiry for one of the following questions: How have the lives of men, women, or children changed as ____(country) industrialized/urbanized since 1950? Encyclopedias, library books, magazine articles, embassies, UNESCO, UNICEF, and interviews with people who have been in the country since 1950 can be used to obtain information. Critically reflect upon any biases in or limitations to your data sources.

9. Write a radio announcement to encourage either individuals or industries to move to your city.

10. Read biographies of people who grew up in rural and urban environments. How did their roots in an urban or rural setting affect their careers and their values?

High School

1. Make a photographic essay of life in a city near you.

2. Research the urban experience for an ethnic group in a particular city. Obtain population data from census reports. Identify churches or businesses that have been part of that community for a long time and find out what you can from their records.

3. Read several different science fiction writers' descriptions of future cities, and write an essay in which you evaluate which characteristics you think are the most and least probable.

4. In a library, read microfiche copies of old newspapers. Identify historical urban problems, and compare them to current ones.

5. Take a single urban problem, and find out how several different cities around the world are coping with it.

6. Reading maps from different time periods, describe urbanization in your state or for a country.

7. Compare prices for groceries in some small grocery stores in a city with those found in the suburbs. Prepare charts showing your information.

8. Visit a courtroom in an urban area and one in a suburb. Write up your observations and generalizations.

9. Analyze speeches made by politicians or political party platforms in terms of their implications for urban dwellers.

In selecting among alternative futures for our urbanized world, citizens must be able to predict consequences of actions, and select those that uphold their values. In order to do that, they must be able to identify and to weigh values. For elementary and middle school students, stories about people living in cities around the world should serve as a basis for values discussions. The values tree, developed for the *Citizenship Decision-Making* curriculum project,[5] is useful for helping students to identify the problem (tree trunk), the possible alternative actions (lowest branches), and their corresponding positive and negative consequences (highest branches). Once students have specified the possible consequences, they should reflect upon the values that each supports. The final step in the discussion should be to ask students what they would do and why. Choice and justification should always follow analysis.

The use of role play is a good way to make apparently remote value dilemmas more concrete for students. This is particularly important when studying urban life in past time periods or in cities one has not seen. In order to conduct a role play, the teacher should set the scene with the specific time, location, and information about events leading up to the scene. The situation should be open-ended and should present an interpersonal conflict. Students should have the opportunity to re-enact the scene several different ways before they compare and contrast alternatives and resulting consequences. (See *Role Playing for Social Values* by Fannie and George Shaftel[6] for more information on the use of role playing for value analysis.) Again choosing and justifying should follow analysis, and students should reflect upon what their decisions show that they value.

While a decision tree and role playing can also be used effectively at the high school level, teachers often feel more comfortable having students analyze value dilemmas in newspaper articles, editorials, letters to the editor, or excerpts from student textbooks. Today's newspaper story, "Mayor Requests Tax Increase for Police Salaries," could be discussed through the following sequence of questions: What is the conflict here? Who has said or done what? What hypotheses do you have about what various people value? What might happen if each of the alternatives were carried out? What values are supported by the alternatives? What do you think should be done and why? What does that show about your values?

Textbook descriptions about problems that faced urban populations in the past can similarly be analyzed by a shift to the following question: "If you were there, what do you think you would have supported and why?" Students will note that their decision differs depending on their role because values are influenced by one's position, one's culture, and the times.

The urbanized world offers many possibilities for the systematic analysis of value issues through curriculum units, debates, or individual research projects and position papers. The following list of questions provides only a few examples of the multitude of issues for which students should consider alternatives, consequences, and supporting values:

1. Is busing a good way to achieve integration?
2. Should suburban residents who work in the city pay a tax to the city?
3. Should welfare programs be expanded?
4. Should arts and sports centers in cities be subsidized by state or federal income tax?
5. Should ethnic holidays be city holidays?
6. Should any employees be exempt from receiving the minimum wage or paying social security?
7. Should city workers be able to strike?

The NCSS *Curriculum Guidelines* note that whatever students of the social studies learn should impel them to apply their knowledge, abilities, and value commitments toward the improvement of the human condition through social participation. Youth are more likely to work actively to improve society when they are adults if they begin early to develop attitudes and abilities supportive of such action. Social participation, like thinking, is developed through practice. Social participation for children, as with adults, should follow from the reflective, systematic analysis of an issue, and it should be voluntary. Below are some possible social action activities that could be undertaken by students to improve urban life today, while they are developing abilities that they will use as adult social actors in the future:

1. After studying about life in cities around the world, prepare a scrapbook or write a storybook about what you have learned. Read it to some younger children.
2. Write a newspaper, prepare a brochure, or design posters to bring attention to an urban issue that people in your community can do something about. Circulate your material in the community.

3. Form a "get-out-the-vote" committee that distributes candidate or issue information sheets, provides maps, arranges for transportation, and provides free babysitters for voters in an urban area.

4. Conduct an oral history project about the personal meaning of *urbanization*. Interview people who moved from a rural to an urban area about their reasons for moving, changes in their lives when they moved, and what they feel the advantages and disadvantages of urban life are. Contribute the audio tapes or transcripts of them to your school library.

5. Take turns with some other students observing at city council meetings or synthesizing newspaper articles about city council meetings or calling a League of Women Voters observer after each meeting to get a report. Report your information in the school newspaper, to government classes, or on posters at community centers.

6. Learn Spanish or teach Spanish to someone who does not already speak it.

7. Tutor a student who is having difficulty in school.

8. Attend a church service of an ethnic group other than your own.

9. Visit a Salvation Army or Goodwill Industries center or an urban mission to find out what they are doing to improve life for urban dwellers. Find out how you and other students can help. Share your information.

10. Prepare a slide–tape presentation on "Urbanization: A Global Process" for your school media center using photographs from cities around the world.

Clearly there is much that social studies classes can do to help students understand the complexities of urbanization and to develop in them the knowledge, abilities, values, and commitments that they will need not only to live in an urbanized world but also to improve it. In order to support these goals, teachers will need opportunities for in-service experiences in urban sites, they will need information about urbanization in the developing nations, and they will need up-to-date materials on global urbanization. Parents and school boards should provide opportunities for suburban youth to experience the city, and speakers should be brought into the schools to explain how urbanization has affected them. Working together, educators and community members can prepare youth for the urbanized world of the 1980's.

REFERENCES

1. Wiley, Karen B. *The Status of Pre-College Science, Mathematics, and Social Science Education: 1955–1975.* Social Science Education, Vol. 3. Boulder, Colo.: Social Science Education Consortium, 1979.

2. Wisniewski, Richard, editor. *Teaching About Life in the City.* Forty-Second Yearbook of the National Council for the Social Studies. Washington, D.C.: the Council, 1972.

3. Osborn, Richard. "Revision of the NCSS Social Studies Curriculum Guidelines." *Social Education* 43: 262–278; 1979.

4. Banks, James A. *Teaching Strategies for the Social Studies.* Reading, Mass.: Addison-Wesley, 1977.

5. La Raus, Roger, and Remy, Richard C. *Citizenship Decision-Making.* Reading, Mass.: Addison-Wesley, 1978.

6. Shaftel, Fannie, and Shaftel, George. *Role Playing for Social Values.* Englewood Cliffs, N.J.: Prentice-Hall, 1967.

CHAPTER 8

Global Education

Dorothy J. Skeel

Recently a second-grade child, when asked to draw his picture of the world, drew a house with an apple tree in the front yard and at the top of the page, a globe on a pedestal. His perception of the world—my home is here and the rest of the world is on the globe. Another second grader chose to represent her view of the world as puzzle pieces that fit together, green pieces representing countries surrounded by blue water. A world view is a strange and puzzling concept for young children to perceive. How will they perceive that world as they grow older?

Why a chapter on global education in a book devoted to social studies education in the 1980's? One could easily argue that it shouldn't be here, but rather it is understood within the very concept and definition of social studies. It is an integral part, an attitude that permeates all of the social studies—an attitude that suggests that the whole must be considered when viewing the world, tackling its problems, or relating to its people. Whether it is interdependence or dependence, the world's resources—water, air, mineral, and agricultural—must be shared by the world's people, a reality that many wish to deny. The use and misuse of those resources affects us all. That is often where the argument begins: Who is going to control those resources? Some critics would contend that global education advocates a world government to control

these resources. However, for most, global education means, first, an awareness of the reality that the world's resources are limited, that the world's people are dependent on one another politically and economically, and that the world's problems are complex and will require cooperation by all if they are to be solved.

Jayne Millar Wood indicates that as the world has progressed since World War II, with more than 100 nations gaining political independence, global life expectancy has improved, the standard of living has moved upward, and science and technology have revolutionized our lives. She observes that with these advances a multitude of new global problems—social, economic, and environmental—"have developed which cannot be solved by nations in isolation from one another. International cooperation, especially *scientific and technological* cooperation is essential if these widespread and persistent problems are to be solved in the future."[1]

To develop an awareness of the foregoing global realities, there is, second, the need to acquire knowledge about the world's problems. For example: (1) the current world population is 4 billion with the possibility of doubling that number in 40 years; (2) there may be a depletion of vital energy resources in 35 years; (3) although 75 percent of the world's population live in Africa, Latin America, and Asia, they receive only 20 percent of the world's income, 12 percent of its industrial output, and less than 5 percent of its scientific and technological potential; (4) food production per capita has lagged behind population for the last nine years.[2]

A third need, possibly the most difficult, is for the reexamination of values and the reordering of priorities. That the world's resources are expendable, that the current rate of energy use cannot continue, that human energy may need to replace some mechanization, and that fuel alternatives may be required so that petroleum can be used for medical and material by-products are all examples of issues that should be raised.

A fourth need is for the development of skills that will permit (1) analysis and evaluation of information about the world from a global perspective, (2) decision making that recognizes that the consequences of those decisions extend far beyond local communities, (3) making thoughtful judgments about their actions, and (4) hypothesizing solutions to problems.

When should global education begin? As early as possible. Children quickly learn stereotypes about other peoples and, by the middle grades, respond less positively to things that are different. A child's perception of the world is uniquely his/her own. Developing an awareness of where other countries are located and of their relative distance from the students helps them to achieve a spatial perception of the world. In turn, this perception helps them to understand how they are a part of that world—how they fit in. Also important is the recognition that people living in other parts of the world view that world from a different perspective.

What can a teacher do? First, ask yourself some questions:

1. Do I have sufficient knowledge about the world's problems—population, food supply, energy resources, land use, distribution of wealth, technological developments?

2. Do I understand the problems and aspirations of the developed and developing nations?

3. Do I have knowledge about theories being advanced (for example, by Buckminster Fuller, Harlan Cleveland, and Barbara Ward) to solve problems from a world perspective?

4. Do I have the skills necessary to introduce a problems approach (inquiry and analysis, simulation, role playing, case studies) to students in a variety of ways?

5. Do I have the skills necessary to introduce the analysis of conflicting value systems?

6. Do I have the human relations skills to work effectively with students from all racial and cultural groups?

7. Am I aware of the resources and materials available to assist me in teaching global concepts?

Depending upon your responses to the above questions, you will need to equip yourself with the necessary knowledge and skills to implement global ideas in your classroom. However, as important as the knowledge and skills are, unless you have (1) acquired an attitude that recognizes the need for global education and (2) developed an atmosphere in your classroom that fosters ideas of global living, it is doubtful that your implementation will be successful.

What classroom strategies and activities can a teacher utilize to help students acquire the necessary knowledge and skills and develop the attitudes and values that will permit them to participate as effective citizens of a global society? There are numerous ways to approach global education in the classroom—a conceptual approach, a topical approach, a problems approach, and an issues approach—depending upon the age and experience of the children. You will need to decide what approach is most effective for you. The strategies and activities suggested here will be organized around the four previously stated goals for global education.

1. *To develop an awareness of the reality that the world's resources are limited, that the world's people are dependent on one another politically and economically, and that because the world's problems are complex, they will require cooperation by all to solve.*

In the earlier grades, it is necessary to develop the foundation for concepts and skills that will be utilized in the later years to analyze issues and solve problems. Therefore, initiate as a beginning (K–2) a series of activities to help students identify needs and wants, recognize how they depend on others to supply their needs and wants, and identify the communities and countries that supply those needs and wants.

Procedure: The lesson would be divided into several days or longer, depending upon the experience of the children. Have students think of all the things that they used prior to arriving at school. List these things on newsprint. Are there things that we can group together (food, clothing, transportation, shelter)? What would we call these groups? Are there things that we could get along without? Cross these out. What would we call those things remaining? (Needs) What can we call the things we crossed out? (Wants) Where do these things come from? Distribute magazines and ask children to find one "needs" and one "wants"; also identify the place where they were made or grown. Have large charts labeled with *Needs* and *Wants*. Have children place their pictures on the appropriate charts. Conduct a discussion to determine if students agree with the choices of their classmates.

Depending on the level and experience of the children, locate places on a map of the United States or the world where the products are grown or made. Talk about how the products reach the store where they are bought. Does anyone know what we call it when we depend on others for our wants and needs? Can you think of anything that might happen that would cause us not to get the things we need (not enough money, strike)? Is there anything that might happen where the product is made or grown?

As a follow-up, ask children to look for needs and wants at home. Determine by the label where they were made or grown. You may choose to make a display of such items.

Upper-level students need help in developing the concept of the whole and of how the people and resources of the world are divided.

Procedure: Divide the class into the major cultures of the world to provide a microcosm. Have each group research its respective culture so that each can understand and present the perspective of its culture. Next, help students visualize their own American culture, which makes up a small proportion of the world's population but uses a large portion of the world's resources. (The United States has about 6 percent of the world's population, but it uses 30 percent of the earth's energy and has approximately 34 percent of the world's wealth.) To dramatize the situation, have the class divide into groups according to population and wealth. Set the desks apart to represent the continents of Asia, Africa, North America, South America, and Europe. In a class of 30, place 15 on the continent of Asia, 5 on Europe, 3 on Africa, 3 on North America, and 4 on South America. Have 30 pieces of candy represent the entire wealth of the world. Give 14 pieces to the 3 people on North America, 9 pieces to the 5 people on Europe, 3 pieces to the 15 people on Asia, 1 to the 3 people on Africa, and 3 to the 4 people on South America. Have students compare how they felt before and after the wealth was distributed.[3]

Involvement activities are also appropriate at the secondary level.

Procedure: Arrange the classes so that students can spend a day together and explain that their food will be supplied and, therefore, they should not eat before arriving. Serve a cup of tea and a small bowl of rice for breakfast. Provide the same meal for lunch and dinner but in the evening include watery soup or some fruit. Students should not leave the room, but for necessity. Debrief the activity by focusing on the feelings of hunger, boredom, and frustration.[4]

2. *To acquire knowledge about the world's problems, such as population, energy, distribution of wealth and resources, food supply, and pollution.*

Any one of these problems offers extensive content and activities for the curriculum. However, it is impossible to deal with all problems in a limited space, so the pollution problem will be utilized.

In the earlier grades, students must conceptualize the meaning of pollution.

Procedure: Have the children throw their scrap paper on the floor for one day, or longer if necessary, for understanding. Be sure to leave time at the end of the day for sufficient debriefing. Have the children look at the room. How do they feel? Are there any problems caused? Bring the paper together. How much is there? Was some thrown away unnecessarily? How can we conserve? Have the children visualize the amount of waste there is in their whole school. What does their experience suggest about the amount of waste in the schools of the community, state, country, and world?

A problem-solving situation may be the best approach for older students.

Procedure: Set up a situation whereby the local community has to decide whether to permit a paper mill to build a plant in their area. The plant will provide jobs for the people, but will pollute the environment and cause tourists to stay away from the local streams and lakes. Give students role cards with the different viewpoints represented— unemployed person, fisherman, paper mill executive, hotel owner, retired couple. Have students role-play a town council meeting with each of the persons giving his/her argument for/against building the paper mill in the community. Then have the town council make the decision.

At the secondary level, students can investigate the greenhouse effect on the world climate.

Procedure: Present the theory that explains the "greenhouse effect." The burning of fossil fuels such as coal and oil to generate electricity or to power automobiles causes more carbon dioxide to be released into the air. It is absorbed somewhat by oceans, but when land is cleared for agricultural or industrial uses, the earth cannot absorb as much carbon dioxide. As the atmosphere collects more than normal amounts of the gas, it acts as a greenhouse to retain heat. The theory suggests that world temperatures could rise as much as 11°F within the next hundred years.

Have students research the effects that could possibly occur from such a *greenhouse effect.* Also, have students determine what the possible alternatives might be to solve the problem.

3. *To reexamine values and reorder priorities as necessitated by current world conditions.*

Procedure: Give younger students an opportunity to think about making choices among needs and wants. Show students a list like the following: television, soap, refrigerator, bicycle, school, telephone, shoes, rice. Ask them to choose something on the list that they cannot get along without. Also, have them decide which one they would miss the least. Have them discuss why they made the choices.

Procedure: Ask older students to make a survey of the electrical appliances they have in their homes. Find out those that their parents and grandparents had in their homes as children. Ask the members of the family which ones they would be willing to give up to save energy. Keep a record of the appliance use for one week. Try to reduce the family's energy use by one-half during the next week. Discuss which would be the easiest to get along without. Which can be eliminated? Which can be used less?[5]

Procedure: Have secondary students examine some of the following questions:

If we continue to increase our own personal use of energy during the next forty years at the same rate which we have during the past, what will be the consequences? Where will we get the additional energy needed? . . .

What kinds of laws should society make to curb energy use?

Are some groups of people in society—for example the poor—hurt more by strict conservation measures than others?

What are factors in American society that have encouraged extravagant energy use (e.g. advertising)? How have improvements in technology led to energy scarcity?[6]

4. *To develop skills that will permit (1) analysis and evaluation of information about the world to review it from a global perspective, (2) decision making that recognizes that the consequences of those decisions extend far beyond local communities, (3) the making of thoughtful judgments about their actions and the actions of others, and (4) the hypothesizing of solutions to global problems.*

Have young children talk about decisions and the consequences of decisions they have made. Ask them to think of consequences that have affected people other than themselves.

Procedure: Ask students to describe some decisions that they have to make. How do they decide what is the best choice? What are consequences? How do consequences affect decisions? Have the children develop a creative writing activity using one of the following:

1. A Decision I Wished I Would Have Made
2. The Hardest Decisions I Ever Made
3. The Consequences of a Decision I Made
4. A Decision I Would Like Someone Else To Make

Comparing, contrasting, and analytical skills can be sharpened with the following activity for older children.

Procedure: Prepare a transparency with the following information about a country and the comparative data:

INFORMATION ABOUT COUNTRY (X):
COMPARISON OF FACTS

AREA:
Texas:	267,339 sq. mi.
Country (X):	481,350 sq. mi.

POPULATION:
Texas:	11,196,730
Country (X):	5,800,000

POPULATION:
Houston:	1,985,031
City (X):	475,000

DENSITY:
Texas:	42.7/sq. mi.
Country (X):	12.1/sq. mi.

COASTLINE:
Texas:	624 mi.
Country (X):	1,000 mi.

EDUCATION:
Country (X):	about 70% illiterate

PRODUCTS:
Coffee (4th largest producer in world)	Sugar
	Cotton
Fish	Manioc
Corn	Palm oil
Sisal	

MINERALS:
Copper	Phosphate
Manganese	Sulphur
Gold	Diamonds

MANUFACTURING:
Foodstuffs	Cement
Tobacco products	Glass
Chemicals	Cotton textiles

CHIEF EXPORTS:
Coffee	Iron ore
Diamonds	Crude oil

When utilizing the information with the students, uncover each section and ask the following series of questions:

1. As you compare the area and population of this country with those of Texas, what conclusions can you draw?

2. From this limited knowledge of the country, identify any problems you think it might have.

3. What might the comparison of coastlines indicate?

4. What might the statistic on illiteracy indicate about the country?

5. What type of climate do these crops suggest?

6. Are there any discrepancies in the climate suggested by these crops?

7. Do the crops suggest anything about the country's location?

8. Do the products indicate any of the industries in the country?

9. Do the exports suggest anything about the technological advancement in this country?

10. What might be some of the problems facing this country?

11. Do any of these problems suggest possible worldwide implications?

12. How might these problems affect your community?

13. Can you identify this country?

For secondary students you could choose to utilize an article from the newspaper to develop problem-solving skills.

Procedure: Present the following article to students. Analyze the data. Pull out the facts that are known. Identify the problem. Hypothesize solutions to the problem. Have students research their hypotheses to determine if they are feasible.

DROUGHT MAY DRAIN INDIA'S FOOD STOCKS, POSE FAMINE

NEW DELHI (UPI)—The worst drought in 60 years could force India to eat through its entire food stockpile and face nationwide famine for the second time in sixty years, officials said.

Reports of hunger and near-starvation were increasing across the nation of 550 million.

OFFICIALS reported many areas were without drinking water and cattle were on the verge of death in parched grasslands. In some districts, villagers were foraging for roots and pawning jewelry to buy food, according to reports reaching the government.

Much land had hardened into a dry, solid crust and fields lay unplowed, the reports said.

Fuel shortages idled irrigation pumps, worsening the problem.[7]

The preceding learning experiences are only a sample of the types of lessons that students will need if they are going to be prepared to participate as citizens of a global society. More importantly, let us hope that through the acquisition of knowledge and skills, they will develop a better sense of self-worth and, subsequently, a care and concern for all peoples of the world.

REFERENCES

1. Wood, Jayne Millar. "Science and Technology for a Global Society." *Social Education* 43: 420; October 1979.

2. Hesburgh, Theodore M., and Henriot, Peter J. "Science and Technology for Development: The Role of the United States." *Social Education* 43: 436; October 1979.

3. Skeel, Dorothy J. *The Challenge of Teaching Social Studies in the Elementary School.* Santa Monica, Calif.: Goodyear, 1979. p. 185.

4. Wood, Jayne Millar. "Adding a Global Outlook to Our Secondary Curriculum: Classroom Teaching Strategies." *Social Education* 38: 671; November–December 1974.

5. Piel, Joe. "Teaching About Science, Technology and Society in the Social Studies." *Social Education* 43: 448; October 1979.

6. *Ibid.*

7. Taken from the November 15, 1979, *Tennessean,* published in Nashville, Tennessee, by Gannett Publications.

CHAPTER 9

Teaching Basic Skills with Social Studies

Barry K. Beyer

Of all the skills taught in our schools, reading comprehension and writing are two of the most basic. These two skills serve not only as goals of classroom learning but as tools for accomplishing other learning goals as well. And nowhere is the dual role of these skills more pronounced and important than in social studies because reading and writing are the major means of learning and evaluating learning in this subject area. If our youth are (1) to achieve the desired cognitive and affective goals of social studies, they must be able (2) to comprehend, process, and express social studies information, concepts, and precepts through reading and writing. To help students accomplish these two goals better than many now do is a major task facing social studies educators in the 1980's.

This task may not be an especially new one. But the approach that seems to offer the greatest promise in accomplishing it may well be: In order to enhance learning in both social studies subject matter and the basics of reading comprehension and writing, *social studies teachers should make instruction in reading comprehension and writing an integral and systematic part of instruction in all social studies courses, at all grade levels—secondary as well as elementary—and for all students—gifted as well as underachieving.* This chapter explores some reasons and methods for implementing such an instructional program.

TEACHING READING AND WRITING
WITH SOCIAL STUDIES

Over the past few years, educators and others have offered many reasons for teaching reading comprehension and writing in content courses, including the social studies.[1] One of the most obvious reasons for such teaching lies in the fact that increasing numbers of our students, especially at the higher grade levels, simply do not read or write as well as teachers, employers, colleges, universities, parents, and even some students themselves would like.[2] A more compelling, if somewhat selfish, reason—at least for those engaged in social studies teaching—lies in the desire to improve student achievement in social studies; research studies indicate that reading instruction in social studies classes does accomplish this goal, while improving reading at the same time.[3] A third reason is one of simple expediency—if social studies teachers fail to provide such instruction, no one else will, because research, furthermore, suggests that there is much less actual instruction in reading comprehension and writing beyond the fourth grade in our schools than we customarily believe exists.[4]

The most important reason for integrating reading and writing instruction in social studies, however, grows out of the fact that conventional approaches to teaching reading and writing simply don't do the job that really needs to be done. Remedial reading and writing classes serve, at best, the needs of only a relatively few students. Special skills units or core classes generally do not give the needed attention to transfer, reinforcement, and continued follow-up skill instruction in content courses. Grab bags of drills or exercises all too frequently fragment skills learning instead of providing the coherent, systematic instruction so crucial to mastery of basic processes like reading comprehension and writing.

None of these conventional approaches deals satisfactorily with the crux of the reading and writing problem afflicting increasing numbers of our students today. And that problem is this: *There is a gradually growing gap between what most students are required to do and what they can do in reading comprehension and writing as they move upward through the grades.* For too many students this gap becomes almost a chasm by the time they reach the upper secondary grades.[5]

Although many factors contribute to the creation of this gap, two deserve particular notice here. First, this reading/writing gap originates partly as a result of confusion on the part of teachers between skill using and skill teaching. Many teachers—in social studies, as in other subjects —erroneously assume that they are teaching skills merely by requiring students to engage, unguided and uninformed, in learning activities that require the use of these skills to whatever degree the students have mastered them.[6]

This gap also originates in large part from a failure to provide skill instruction in the subject matter courses where these skills are used—including the social studies.[7] Students are introduced to the fundamentals of reading comprehension and writing in the early grades; thereafter, they customarily receive relatively little direct instruction designed to extend their use of these skills in the increasingly sophisticated ways with increasingly complex information, vocabulary, and concepts, and with the increasingly complex and varied learning materials that confront them in the subjects they study in subsequent grades.[8] Students who do not develop the skills necessary to cope with these demands find themselves dropping further and further behind grade-level norms in reading and writing as they move from grade to grade.

Dealing with this situation requires more than remediation for those who have already fallen victim to it. It requires *preventing the development of such a gap in the first place.* For the vast majority of students in social studies we can accomplish this goal by providing systematic, developmental instruction in reading comprehension and writing in all social studies courses at all grade levels in our schools. Teaching reading comprehension and writing in social studies does not mean that social studies teachers must become reading or writing experts, however. Nor does it mean giving up content for skill teaching. What this approach does mean is providing explicit instruction in these processes as they are used to work with content throughout the social studies curriculum.

Research on the nature and teaching of reading comprehension and writing suggests that there is no single "best way" to teach either process.[9] But this same research, as well as exemplary educational practices now in use, does suggest that for such instruction to succeed in social studies, it should meet these three criteria: First, *explicit, systematic instruction and practice* in comprehension and writing using social studies materials, content, and concepts should be provided by social studies teachers. Second, this instruction and practice should be *developmental* within a single course and across all grade levels so that students can refine and extend their competencies in using these skills as they move from one level of learning to another. Finally, instruction in reading and writing in social studies should be *integrated* with each other and with the subject matter with which they are being used; these processes should be used to further content-oriented purposes rather than be taught as ends in themselves.

DEVELOPMENTAL READING COMPREHENSION
IN SOCIAL STUDIES

Improving student reading comprehension in social studies requires more than periodic attention to vocabulary or use of drills in recognizing main ideas or detecting author bias. It involves explicit attention to the entire process of comprehension by instruction that precedes, coincides with, and follows any reading activity. Such instruction ought to provide analogous, as well as equivalent, practice. It should also involve student analysis as well as teacher explanation and demonstration. And, to be most effective, this instruction also ought to go somewhere. To be truly developmental, instruction in reading comprehension must move students gradually from where they are to higher levels of competency and sophistication in terms of skill usage.

The nature of reading comprehension itself offers clues to the planning of potentially useful developmental reading instruction. Reading comprehension involves essentially the ability to understand a message transmitted by print or writing. According to many specialists it consists of understanding (1) what the message says literally, (2) what its author probably means by what is written, and (3) what it means to the reader, given everything else the reader knows about the topic to which it relates, her or his purpose in reading the message, and the context in which it is used.[10] Reading comprehension thus involves, as Nila Banton Smith asserts, giving meaning to a message as well as extracting meaning from it.[11]

Defining reading comprehension in this way suggests that a practical, developmental reading program for social studies should have at least three dimensions: It should (1) help students develop strategies for comprehending what they read, (2) move students from lower levels to higher levels of comprehension, and (3) progress from teacher-directed to student-directed reading. A number of techniques and materials can be pieced together to create such a reading program.

Initially—in the intermediate grades or at the start of a course—students ought to receive instruction in using one or more strategies for reading in social studies. The SQ3R comprehension strategy is one very useful strategy that students can be taught.[12] In essence this strategy requires students to *survey* or *skim* materials to be read in order to gain an overview of the major topics presented, generate *questions* about these topics that they would like answered, and then *read* the material carefully to answer these questions, *reciting* or recording their answers as they proceed. Finally, by way of *review,* students summarize the main points of the material and/or apply these points to new data. This five-step strategy can be used to facilitate comprehension of a map or graph, of a filmstrip or collection of photos, or of an oral presentation, as well as of a text selection, document, or story.

Teachers can provide instruction in the use of SQ3R orally and through the use of written reading guides. The latter can actually provide instruction as well as practice while students engage actively in the study of their social studies content. A reading guide designed to do just this might start as the following excerpt from a guide to a typical American history text:

Step 1

> *Survey* To complete this step of SQ3R, skim the complete assignment quickly. This will help you identify the main topics to be covered in these pages. To find these topics, look at the chapter title, the headlines in large and/or colored print, the first and last paragraphs of the assigned section, and the maps, graphs, charts, and pictures, and their captions. Surveying tells you what the assignment will be about. As you skim Chapter 7, answer these questions:

1. Chapter 7 will include which topic?
   a. The American colonists' decision to declare their independence.
   b. The creation of a federal union.
   c. The start of an American way of life.

2. How do you know that Chapter 7 will include the topic you selected in question 1?
   a. Because it is a caption under a picture.
   b. Because it is the chapter title.
   c. Because it is a headline printed in large letters and in color.

3. Chapter 7 will also deal with which topic?
   a. The growing tensions between Britain and the colonies.
   b. The spread of the Industrial Revolution to America.
   c. A favorable treaty of peace for the victorious Americans.

4. How do you know that the topic selected in question 3 will be included in Chapter 7?————————————————

Instruction on how to complete this step may be provided—as here—by the directions and by questions that involve the student in analyzing how she or he is reading. Questions 2 and 4 exemplify such questions. Furthermore, the multiple-option answers in these items provide implicit guidance in how to complete this reading operation; the existence of an option that corresponds to a phrase in the text signals the rule or identifies the clues that one must follow or look for to engage in this step of comprehending. A complete SQ3R guide presents a series of items similar to the above for each step in this process.

As students master the SQ3R strategy, detailed directions and process questions can gradually be eliminated. Eventually more open-ended guides can replace the multiple-choice format altogether. Such an "open" guide may start by asking students to skim an assigned reading, to list the topics it will cover, and then to write a question or questions that would help them learn more about each topic. Then students can read the assignment carefully to find—and record on the reading guide —information that answers their questions. Finally, students can be asked to pull their reading together by stating the main idea of the material and/or by applying it in a variety of ways to information learned earlier or to new data.[13]

As a second stage in a social studies developmental reading program, perhaps in the middle grades or at the mid-point in a specific course, reading comprehension items can shift in focus from translation-type items to those requiring different levels of comprehension.[14] Such items can progress from those that ask for simple translation—like question 5 below—to those that require interpretation (question 6) and synthesis (question 7), analysis, or evaluation:

5. Where was the first battle between armed colonials and British troops fought?
   a. Saratoga
   b. Lexington
   c. Yorktown

6. The map on p. 102 shows that the fighting during the Revolution—
   a. Occurred at the same time throughout the colonies.
   b. Took place mainly in the southern half of the colonies.
   c. Shifted from the northern colonies to the southern colonies and finally to the middle colonies.

7. Which of the following would be the best overall title for these sections of the text?
   a. How Events Led to a Decision for American Independence
   b. How the Thirteen Colonies Won Independence
   c. How British Colonists Became Americans

Such items can be multiple choice in nature when the teacher wishes to provide instruction in these skills. Or they may be of the true/false/correct type when only practice is desired. Both types may also be interspersed with "How do you know your answer is correct?" questions in multiple choice or completion format to provide students with instructive guidance.

Finally, a developmental reading program in social studies can culminate in the secondary grades with reading activities that show students how, and then require them, to abstract meaning from reading—or viewing or listening—material. Marilyn Buckley Hanf suggests that students produce on a single page a diagram of a reading selection that actually shows by lines the relationships among major ideas, subordinate ideas, reasoning, evidence, and example.[15] Such diagrams—or maps—can be constructed following the structure of the reading being used or according to questions students or teachers wish to ask of the reading. By making such maps, students employ the previously learned strategies and levels of reading comprehension to abstract and synthesize given and new meanings. Such a technique represents a much more sophisticated way of comprehending than does the completion of a multiple-choice reading guide. If social studies students could move toward mastery of this technique as they progress through their courses, they would be much more likely to stay abreast of the increasingly abstract substantive demands of their courses and, thus, they would be less likely to fall below grade-level norms in their abilities to comprehend the instructional materials commonly used in social studies.

DEVELOPMENTAL WRITING IN SOCIAL STUDIES

Writing is a complex cognitive process. It consists essentially of three major operations: (1) thinking up what to write—identifying and inferring relationships among data; (2) composing—choosing what data or reasoning to use, articulating relationships, ordering evidence and arguments, and so on; and (3) evaluating—judging the appropriateness, order, and meaning of these data for purposes of clarity, accuracy, and thoroughness.[16] By using these operations we seek to produce a clearly expressed thought, supported by explicitly interrelated reasoning, evidence, and examples—a thought whose significance is obvious to all. Like reading, writing is an active process in which one learns about a topic while processing information about it.[17]

As in reading, social studies teachers need to provide direct instruction in the basic aspects of writing as they apply to social studies. Of particular importance is instruction in generating and organizing ideas and information through pre-writing, rewriting, and revising activities and instruction.[18] Equally important, however, is the use of writing and instruction in writing in a way that is developmental in structure and purpose.

Student writing in social studies should help students move gradually from descriptive writing about rather specific objects or events to more sophisticated analytical writing about abstract concepts and ideas. Among the elements to be considered part of such an approach, four seem especially basic: (1) the length of the assignment; (2) the writing task; (3) the type of content to be used; and (4) the audience to be addressed.[19] As students move from one course to another, or even through a single course, the tasks, content used, and audiences addressed should become progressively more abstract, impersonal, and general.

A variety of techniques may be easily used to implement such a writing program. For example, writing in intermediate-grade social studies courses might well focus exclusively on single paragraphs; the major task should be to describe or to narrate; the content to be written about should be concrete in nature—such as inventions, events, or people; and the audience addressed might best be students younger than themselves. But as students move into increasingly abstract secondary-level social studies courses—and courses that deal in time, cultural, and generational dimensions quite removed from the present or the concrete—their writing might well move toward a series of paragraphs; their major tasks can be to explain and eventually to persuade; the topics used could be more abstract—dealing with forces such as nationalism, processes such as migration, or ideas such as democracy; and the audiences can be individuals from cultures, time periods, and age levels different from those of the students.

Even within a single social studies course, writing can be developmental. Students in an eighth-grade American history course, for instance, could first write a paragraph describing to a younger brother or sister several events leading up to the American Revolution. Later in the same course they could write similar paragraphs about Shay's Rebellion. Still later, using these two paragraphs as data bases, they could write a paragraph explaining similarities or differences in these events. The sequence could then culminate in another, later paragraph explaining the major purpose of government in general; the ideas generated by this final paragraph could serve as a springboard for study of the Constitution. The principles articulated by this sequence of writing activities could be employed throughout all social studies courses.[20]

INTEGRATING INSTRUCTION IN READING, WRITING, AND SOCIAL STUDIES

Instruction in reading and writing in social studies—to be most effective—must serve to advance rather than to interrupt subject matter learning. Instruction in these basics, as well as instruction in the subject matter, should be neither compartmentalized nor fragmented. Students should receive instruction in reading comprehension when they are required to read in order to accomplish a content purpose. And the same applies to writing.

In fact, reading, writing, and content instruction can be interwoven to advance student understanding and mastery of each, as well as to move a course along from beginning to conclusion. For example, students could skim (a reading skill) a textbook chapter to generate a list of data (a pre-writing technique) about which to write a paragraph. They could then treat the concluding sentences of their paragraphs as hypotheses, rereading the chapter in detail to test the accuracy of these claims as well as to generate new insights. Thus, their writing generates a purpose for reading! Paired or group discussion of evidence could then lead to rewriting of their paragraphs, perhaps from another point of view. Peer evaluation and further revising and rewriting could follow. Throughout this entire sequence, students will be analyzing, discussing, and using subject matter. Ideas developed through this process can become springboards for the study of the next chapter or topic.

It would be erroneous to claim that integrating instruction in reading and writing with social studies would not eat into the time available for "covering" content in our classrooms. But we can minimize such loss of time.[21] By integrating process and subject matter instruction as described above, we can make the same teaching do double duty. Skills teaching and content study can support each other. Whenever students find it necessary to collect information from a text or even a visual or oral presentation, we can provide instruction on how to comprehend. Their discussion and work at these tasks naturally involve them in the content being studied. Writing can be used whenever students customarily now discuss, report, or answer questions in a social studies class. When they do write, we can take the opportunity to provide instruction in writing through appropriate pre-writing, writing, and rewriting activities.

Such instruction need not occur *every* time students read and write. Direct instruction can give way to supervised practice and eventually to student-directed and -initiated study using these skills as a course proceeds and as students move through the curriculum. But by taking advantage of the reading and writing that does or could go on in our classrooms, we can provide instruction in both skills and content—if not quite simultaneously, at least so that they reinforce one another in the accomplishment of larger learning goals.

TEACHING BASIC SKILLS WITH SOCIAL STUDIES

Attention to reading and writing should be a major concern of social studies teachers and curriculum designers in the 1980's. The need for dealing with these basics became dramatically evident during the past decade. We now have an opportunity to meet this need by designing, testing, and implementing systematic, developmental, integrated basic skill programs in all social studies classes at all grade levels. By so doing we can sharply enhance student achievement in social studies knowledge and skills. And, at the same time, we can move in positive fashion not only to reduce the gap in student mastery of these basics but more importantly to assure that such gaps have less likelihood of occurring to begin with. Teaching reading and writing with social studies allows social studies educators to do something that we have not yet done well: to deal constructively with the basic skill and knowledge learning needs of our students. By actively acknowledging the fundamental interrelationships among reading, writing, and subject matter learning, social studies in the 1980's can make a major contribution to the educaton of every child.

REFERENCES

1. See, for example: Herber, Harold. *Teaching Reading in Content Areas.* Englewood Cliffs, N.J.: Prentice-Hall, 1970 (Second edition, 1978).

Laffey, James L., editor. *Reading in the Content Areas.* Newark, Del.: International Reading Association, 1972.

Preston, Ralph, editor. *A New Look at Reading in the Social Studies.* Newark, Del.: International Reading Association, 1969.

Beyer, Barry K. *Back-to-Basics in Social Studies.* Boulder, Colo.: Social Science Education Consortium, Inc., 1977. pp. 7–23.

2. *Reading in America: A Perspective on Two Assessments.* Denver: National Assessment of Educational Progress, 1976.

"Industry Also Finds Johnny Can't Read." *Pittsburgh Press,* July 6, 1976.

Sheils, Merrill. "Why Johnny Can't Write." *Newsweek,* December 8, 1975. pp. 58–65.

"Young Writers OK in Simple Tasks, in Trouble on Complex." *NAEP Newsletter* X: 5–6; January 1977.

3. See the following studies: Leggitt, Dorothy. "Measuring Progress in Working Skills in Ninth Grade Civics." *School Review* 42: 676–687; November 1934.

Studies by Fay (1950), Krantz (1957), Hilson (1961), Schiller (1963), and Sepp (1965) [cited in: Estes, Thomas H. "Reading in the Social Studies—A Review of Research Since 1950." *Reading in the Content Areas.* (Edited by James L. Laffey.) Newark, Del.: International Reading Association, 1972. pp. 178–183.]

4. Lundstrum, John. "Reading in the Social Studies: A Preliminary Analysis of Recent Research." *Social Education* 40: 11–12; January 1976.

Haynes, Elizabeth F. "Using Research in Preparing to Teach Writing." *English Journal* 67: 82; January 1978.

Michaels, Melvin. "Subject Reading Improvement—A Neglected Teaching Responsibility." *Journal of Reading* IX: 16–20; October 1965.

5. Hunter, Carman St. John, and Harman, David. *Adult Illiteracy in the United States.* New York: Ford Foundation, 1979.

"Colleges Bolstering Courses to Improve Writing Ability." *New York Times,* February 7, 1977.

6. Herber, Harold. *op. cit.* pp. vi–viii.

7. Gross, Richard E. "The Status of the Social Studies in the Public Schools of the United States." *Social Education* 41: 199; March 1977.

Lundstrum, John. *loc. cit.*

Haynes, Elizabeth F. *loc. cit.*

8. Karlin, Robert. "What Does Research in Reading Reveal About Reading and the High School Student?" *English Journal* 58: 386–395; March 1969.

Haynes, Elizabeth F. *loc. cit.*

9. Lundstrum, John. *op. cit.* pp. 10–18.

Haynes, Elizabeth F. *op. cit.* pp. 82–88.

Williams, Palmer S. *Selected Techniques for Teaching Writing: A Handbook for Teachers, Grades 4–12.* Durham, N.C.: Moore Publishing Company, 1977. pp. 7–35.

Estes, Thomas H. *op. cit.* pp. 177–187.

10. Herber, Harold. *op. cit.* pp. 62–63. (Second edition, pp. 43–55.)

Gray, William S. "The Major Aspects of Reading." *Sequential Development of Reading Abilities.* (Edited by Helen M. Robinson.) Chicago: University of Chicago Press, 1960. p. 17.

Lundstrum, John P., and Taylor, Bob L. *Teaching Reading in the Social Studies.* Newark, Del.: International Reading Association, 1978. pp. 40–41.

11. Smith, Nila Banton. *Reading Instruction for Today's Children.* Englewood Cliffs, N.J.: Prentice-Hall, 1963. p. 264.

12. Robinson, F.P. *Effective Study.* Revised edition. New York: Harper & Brothers, 1961.

Wark, David M., editor. "Survey Q3R: System or Superstition?" *College and Adult Reading, III–IV.* Minneapolis: North Central Reading Association, 1965. pp. 161–170.

13. For examples of such reading guides, see: Beyer, Barry K. "Improving Reading in History: A Teaching Approach." *The History and Social Science Teacher* 15; Winter 1980.

14. For examples and guidelines, see: Herber, Harold. *op. cit.* (Second edition.) pp. 55–71.

Lundstrum, John P., and Taylor, Bob L. *op. cit.* pp. 46–47.

Beyer, Barry K. *Teaching Thinking in Social Studies.* Columbus, Ohio: Charles E. Merrill Publishing Co., Inc., 1979. pp. 244–248.

Beyer, Barry K. *Back-to-Basics.* pp. 24–46.

15. Hanf, Marilyn Buckley. "Mapping: A Technique for Translating Reading into Thinking." *Journal of Reading* 14: 225–230, 270; January 1971.

16. Flower, Linda S., and Hayes, John R. "Problem Solving Strategies and the Writing Process." *College English* 39: 449–461; December 1977.

Neill, Shirley Boes. "How to Improve Student Writing." *American Education,* October 1976. pp. 6–12.

17. Baker, Sheridan. "Writing as Discovery." *ADE Bulletin* 54: 34–37; November 1974.

Emig, Janet. "Writing as a Mode of Learning." *College Composition and Communication* 28: 122–133; May 1977.

Van Nostrand, A.D. "Writing and the Generation of Knowledge." *Social Education* 43: 178–180; March 1979.

18. *Write/Rewrite: An Assessment of Revision Skills.* Denver: National Assessment of Educational Progress, 1977.

Beyer, Barry K. "Pre-Writing and Rewriting to Learn." *Social Education* 43: 187–189, 197; March 1979.

19. Britton, James, and others. *The Development of Writing Abilities (11–18).* London: Macmillan Education, 1975.

Egan, Kieran. *Educational Development.* New York: Oxford University Press, 1979. pp. 9–89.

20. Brostoff, Anita. "Good Assignments Lead to Good Writing." *Social Education* 43: 184–186; March 1979.

Giroux, Henry. "Teaching Content and Thinking Through Writing." *Social Education* 43: 190–193; March 1979.

Ventre, Raymond. "Developmental Writing: Social Studies Assignments." *Social Education* 43: 181–183, 197; March 1979.

21. For practical ways to achieve this goal, see: Fader, Daniel. *The New Hooked on Books.* New York: Berkley Publishing Co., 1976. pp. 7–43.

Beyer, Barry K., and Brostoff, Anita. "The Time It Takes: Managing/Evaluating Writing and Social Studies." *Social Education* 43: 194–197; March 1979.

CHAPTER 10

Now, More Than Ever . . . Decision-Making and Related Skills

Anna S. Ochoa

The purpose of the social studies is to develop informed, ethical, and effective citizens. In today's world these citizens should be dedicated to improving the condition of both their society and the global community. We must keep in mind, however, that as individuals we do not and, in fact, cannot function effectively as citizens until we have established a sense of our own identities as well as a sense of connectedness or integration with others. Social studies, therefore, needs to be concerned with the private self as well as the public self. This statement of purpose guides my selection of the significant skills that require the attention of social studies teachers during the 1980's. The most essential of these skills is that of decision making. Significant, related skills are critical thinking, group effectiveness, and participation.

In presenting each of these skills, the following two questions will be addressed:

1. What is meant by the category—i.e., decision-making, critical-thinking, group effectiveness, or participation skills?

2. Why is this category of skills significant?

DECISION-MAKING SKILLS

What Are Decision-Making Skills?

Since it is doubtful that anyone could say it better, the description of decision making that is used here is taken from the first chapter by Cassidy and Kurfman of the Forty-Seventh Yearbook of the National Council for the Social Studies (NCSS):

> Decision making can be defined as the making of reasoned choices from among several alternatives. Reasoned choices are choices based on judgments which are consistent with the decision-maker's values. They are also choices based on relevant, sound information. So conceived, decision making is not limited to considerations of public issues, such as for whom to vote, or whether to support high-rise developments in one's community. It includes decisions of a personal nature as well, such as what to do about the threatening person on the playground, whether to buy a car, or which college to attend. The common characteristic of all instances of true decision making, whether they are personal or public decisions, is the existence of alternative courses of action which require judgments in terms of one's values.[1]

This definition emphasizes that decision making is directly tied to one's values, that it is both personal and public in nature, and that the decision-making process needs to be reflective and thoughtful. This decision-making process is illustrated in Figure 1.[2]

This model of decision making was selected for several reasons. First, it is useful for both personal and public issues. Second, the model

FIGURE 1

STAGES IN THE DECISION-MAKING PROCESS

FACTS / GENERALIZATIONS

Identify Decision Occasions and Their Alternatives:
a. Define the decision to be made.
b. Identify the goals of the decision-maker.
c. Identify available alternatives.

Examine and Evaluate Decision Alternatives:
a. Examine the probable outcomes of each alternative.
b. Evaluate and rank the alternatives.

Decide and Reflect on the Decision:
a. Select an alternative.
b. Implement the plan of action.
c. Assess the results of action.
d. Consider recycling the process.

VALUES / FEELINGS

honors the importance of knowledge (facts and generalizations) and, in this way, fosters reflective and informed rather than impulsive decision making. Third, and just as important, the model accepts the role of both feelings and values. In this way it is holistic because it taps not only the intellectual but also the emotional dimensions of human beings.

However, one criticism is warranted here. This model appears to assume that one value is as good as another. It does not explicitly encourage the user to establish a linkage between his or her goals and specific higher values. For example, let's assume that someone is making a decision about whether to support the Equal Rights Amendment. The occasion for the decision is a forthcoming election. In examining what her goals are, the person in question decides that her goal is to please her friends. Since they are supporting ERA, she will, too. In the described decision-making model, her argument is sufficient. Not at this point, or at any other, is the decision-maker required to reconcile his or her goals with a higher value such as "human dignity." When users of the model are later involved in evaluating and examining alternatives, they are encouraged to relate the alternatives to their values; but, again, no questions are asked about the merit of those values. Yet many, if not most, thoughtful people would agree that respect for others or the desire to improve the human condition (both of these are recastings of the value of human dignity) will be as essential in the unknown of tomorrow's world as it is in making decisions about today's complex social issues. Psychological integrity may be served when individuals reconcile their decisions with their own values, regardless of whether or not those values are self-serving, but this process does not foster social responsibility. Without social responsibility, the concept of citizenship is rendered meaningless and the fate of society is doomed.

This weakness of the model is substantial. Without a guiding value such as human dignity, the model is ethically neutral. It is relativistic, and permits selfish and even destructive solutions. Nonetheless, overall the Cassidy–Kurfman process has considerable worth and the remedy to the weakness just described is a relatively simple one. With the slight modifications that appear in Figure 2, the model becomes one that more explicitly guides socially responsible decisions.

Cassidy and Kurfman appropriately caution that the model is not as simple as it seems. While laid out as a step-by-step process, decision making is not linear. Each part of the process impinges on the others. Nonetheless, the model provides a very useful tool for teachers and students in social studies classrooms.

FIGURE 2

STAGES IN THE DECISION-MAKING PROCESS

FACTS / GENERALIZATIONS

VALUES / FEELINGS

Identify Decision Occasions and Their Alternatives:
a. Define the decision to be made.
b. Identify the goals of the decision-maker (relate these goals to human dignity).*
c. Identify available alternatives.

Examine and Evaluate Decision Alternatives:
a. Examine the probable outcomes of each alternative.
b. Evaluate and rank the alternatives (relate the alternatives to human dignity).*

Decide and Reflect on the Decision:
a. Select an alternative (justify it in terms of human dignity).*
b. Implement the plan of action.
c. Assess the results of action.
d. Consider recycling the process.

*As adapted by the author.

Steps of the Model. Readers owe it to themselves to read the Cassidy and Kurfman chapter in the 47th NCSS Yearbook and to become well acquainted with their decision-making model. However, a brief description of each of the steps is provided here. Statements in brackets represent modifications by this author.

1. *IDENTIFY DECISION OCCASIONS AND THEIR ALTERNATIVES*

   a. *Define the Decision To Be Made*

   This step involves analysis after the decision-maker becomes aware that an occasion for a decision exists. Cassidy and Kurfman emphasize the need for knowledge at this point so that the right questions are asked. The decision should be described explicitly.

   b. *Identify the Goals of the Decision-Maker* [*Relate These Goals to Human Dignity*][3]

   At this step the decision-maker identifies his or her goals and relates these goals to the value of human dignity (respect for others, concern for the improvement of the human condition, etc.). Here, it is important to clarify one's goals and be able to defend them in terms of human dignity.

c. *Identify Available Alternatives*

Here, the decision-maker identifies as many alternatives as possible so that a wide range of options exists. Brainstorming is a technique that is useful at this stage. An important caution is that no assessment of the alternatives should be made at this time for fear of delimiting possible options. This process entails creative as well as critical thinking and is often aided by information that can facilitate the development of a number of alternatives.

2. *EXAMINE AND EVALUATE DECISION ALTERNATIVES*

a. *Examine the Probable Outcomes of Each Alternative*

All possible short-term and long-term consequences for each alternative are now identified. Knowledge becomes most useful here.

b. *Evaluate and Rank the Alternatives* [*Relate the Alternatives to Human Dignity*]

At this point, each alternative and its consequences are assessed. While there may be several criteria by which to judge these alternatives, one needs to be the extent to which human dignity is enhanced if that particular decision is made. The alternatives are then ranked. It is here that the decision-maker attempts to reconcile personal feelings and values with social responsibility.

3. *DECIDE AND REFLECT ON THE DECISION*

a. *Select an Alternative* [*Justify It in Terms of Human Dignity*]

This is the point in the process at which the decision is made and a plan for implementation considered. Justification in terms of human dignity is created.

b. *Implement the Plan of Action*

While this step appears to be obvious and logical following the making of a decision, often for reasons of fear, individuals vacillate about or avoid taking action.

c. *Assess the Results of Action*

Here, the outcomes of the action are assessed, and a determination is made as to whether the action and its underlying decision contribute to the goals of the decision-maker (and enhance human dignity). Further, the entire process of making the decision is reviewed to identify strengths and weaknesses.

d. *Consider Recycling the Process*

Since most decisions are not irreversible, the opportunity to go back through the process and select another alternative should be considered.

Embracing decision making as a major goal of the social studies makes other demands on the social studies curriculum. The matter of *knowledge* to illuminate decision making has already been mentioned briefly. A focus on decision making does not de-emphasize knowledge. In fact, such a focus emphasizes the need for valid and powerful knowledge about the social conditions that represent the context of decision making. In addition, decision making entails a number of other skills. Some of these have been discussed in the previous chapter. Others will be discussed here. Cassidy and Kurfman[4] provide one framework (Figure 3) for identifying such skills.

FIGURE 3

DECISION-MAKING SKILL OBJECTIVES

Direct Information-Gathering Skills

A. Asking questions
    1. Asking who, what, how
    2. Reformulating questions

B. Observing
    1. Using all senses
    2. Interpreting cues
    3. Deciding which senses to use
    4. Making inferences

C. Listening
    1. Paying attention
    2. Paraphrasing
    3. Asking clarifying questions

Skills for Gathering Information from Prepared Sources

A. Reading
    1. Clarifying the purpose
    2. Identifying word meanings
    3. Recalling or recognizing
    4. Summarizing and inferring

FIGURE 3 (Continued)

B. Using maps
   1. Interpreting symbols
   2. Determining directions
   3. Determining distances
   4. Selecting appropriate maps
C. Using graphs and tables
   1. Identifying title and axis variables
   2. Extracting facts
   3. Drawing inferences

Thinking Skills

A. Analyzing–Synthesizing
   1. Identifying the elements in the occasion for decision
   2. Comparing with analogous decision occasions
   3. Defining the issue(s) to be decided
   4. Identifying two or more possible decision alternatives
   5. Identifying values of the decision-maker(s)
   6. Formulating a plan of action
B. Applying–Predicting
   1. Applying information from analogous occasions
   2. Recalling relevant "if, then" generalizations
   3. Predicting the probable immediate and long-range consequences of each alternative
C. Evaluating–Judging
   1. Judging the desirability of projected consequences
   2. Evaluating each alternative in terms of consequences
   3. Comparing alternatives in terms of strengths and weaknesses
   4. Evaluating the chosen alternative in terms of its actual consequences

The Significance of Decision-Making Skills

Experience with and competence in decision making are of paramount importance. This condition has always been true. Decisions shape our personal lives and the lives of those around us, as well as the quality of life in our society; and with increasing frequency, our decisions influence the lives of people in other nations, as their decisions influence ours. In a democratic nation, special importance attaches to decision making if the consent-of-the-governed principle is to be realized.

Decisions can be, and are, made whimsically, thoughtlessly, and selfishly. Conversely, with guidance and experience, people can, and do, learn to make decisions seriously, reflectively, and responsibly. It is the latter goal that needs to be embraced by social studies teachers if we are to have any hope for the next generation of citizens.

Too often social studies programs are preoccupied with the learning of facts or even concepts and generalizations. Skills like map reading seem never to be ignored. Yet decision making occurs only in some social studies classrooms, certainly not all. While the understanding of major ideas is important, such understanding is only important to the extent that it enriches our decision making and not as an end in itself. The social studies profession has spent far too much time and effort identifying appropriate knowledge for the curriculum, while giving only scant attention to the process of teaching young people to make socially responsible decisions.

Toward Socially Responsible Decision Making

If attention to decision making is to contribute to the development of socially responsible adults, social studies teachers will need to bite a difficult bullet. Specifically, decision making will have to be taught in the context of a deep commitment to the value of human dignity, which means equal access to the rights and responsibilities associated with membership in a culture or even in the global community.

For too long, many in the social studies have given lip service to a value neutrality in the curriculum. They have argued that it is not important *what* young people think; rather it is important *that* they think. Such a stance is not acceptable. It is not socially useful, nor is it responsible. As the world's population increases, the amount of livable space and other resources decrease; and as we, as individuals and as a nation, become increasingly interdependent and in some cases even dependent, the decisions we make must be guided by a concern for the welfare of others, not just ourselves.

Human dignity is a universal value. It is embraced by all religions. It is the principle that underlies such democratic values as freedom, equality, and justice. Because it is subject to wide interpretation, it is possible for people who hold this value to find themselves on opposing sides of a particular argument. For instance, the environmentalist who wants to impose heavy fines on an industrial installation can invoke it in the name of harm to human health. On the same issue, an industrial representative can tie it to the argument that increased jobs improve the quality of life in the community. In spite of such diverse applications, it is still useful because it requires that the decision-maker be concerned with the well-being of others, and it prevents him or her from being satisfied with arguments that are purely selfish. None of the above should be construed as a carte blanche to indoctrination. Each student must have the right to make whatever decision he/she sees fit, but the justification for the decision must be cast in terms of human dignity. The future will not tolerate less.

The remainder of this chapter will give attention to three kinds of skills: critical-thinking, group effectiveness, and participation skills. To the author, all three are inextricably related to decision making.

CRITICAL-THINKING SKILLS

What Are Critical-Thinking Skills?

Critical thinking has, by and large, been casually discussed in the social studies literature. Everybody supports it, but few, if any, specify its meaning. A most comprehensive analysis of the concept was presented by Robert Ennis in 1967.[5] Unfortunately, its application to the classroom has not followed. Ennis defines critical thinking as "the correct assessing of statements." He then presents its 12 aspects, which appear below. As the reader works his or her way through this list, it should become clear that the emphasis lies in analytic skills and logical reasoning. These 12 aspects are as follows:

1. Grasping the meaning of a statement.
2. Judging whether there is ambiguity in a line of reasoning.
3. Judging whether certain statements contradict each other.
4. Judging whether a conclusion follows necessarily.
5. Judging whether a statement is specific enough.
6. Judging whether a statement is actually the application of a certain principle.
7. Judging whether an observation statement is reliable.
8. Judging whether an inductive conclusion is warranted.
9. Judging whether the problem has been identified.
10. Judging whether something is an assumption.
11. Judging whether a definition is adequate.
12. Judging whether a statement made by an alleged authority is acceptable.

The Significance of Critical-Thinking Skills

Space does not allow a full elaboration of each of the 12 aspects of critical thinking. Nonetheless, it is clear that the skills involved enhance the capabilities of any decision-maker, regardless of whether the decision is personal or public.

As citizens living in a global age, the need for such skills is heightened. All citizens will be confronted daily by transnational problems, the claims of national and international political figures, and the information glut perpetrated by the media. Whether they are victims of this complex environment or viable actors in it will depend in large part on their ability to judge the merit of the statements presented to them.

All teachers, but teachers of social studies in particular, need to provide carefully planned opportunities for students to develop these skills. Knowledge alone, while necessary, is not sufficient. Without the skills to effectively use knowledge, decision-makers must rely on their best hunches. For the multifaceted future, hunches are not good enough.

GROUP EFFECTIVENESS SKILLS

What Are Group Effectiveness Skills?

In the context of citizenship education, group effectiveness skills are those competencies that permit maximal satisfaction of both individual and group goals.

Social psychologists have contributed most substantially to our understanding of group process. The skills described below are derived from the conception presented by David W. Johnson and Frank P. Johnson.[6] These skills include:

1. Clarifying goals in terms of the best match between the goals of individuals and the goals of the group.

2. Communicating ideas and feelings accurately and effectively.

3. Sharing participation and leadership among group members. Such sharing contributes to the involvement and satisfaction of all members of the group.

4. Matching decision-making procedures with the situation.

5. Sharing power and influence throughout the group. These dimensions should be based on expertise, ability, and access to information, and not on authority.

6. Encouraging and negotiating conflict. This factor includes the use of minority opinion and recognizes that conflict promotes involvement and creativity.

7. Building group cohesion. The emphasis here is on acceptance, trust, and support among group members.

8. Exhibiting problem-solving ability.

9. Building interpersonal effectiveness.

The Significance of Group Effectiveness Skills

Decisions are often made in groups. Whether the group is Congress, a city council, or the board of directors of an organization, its effectiveness depends upon the skills that are reflected in its members' decisions. If group members are sensitive to the demands of effective group process, the chances of success are substantially enhanced.

Citizens participate in many kinds of groups. These groups include the family and friendship groups at the most personal level; organizational groups within a business, corporation, agency, or union; and political groups as represented by political parties or county commissions. Social studies education has given far too little attention to building these essential skills. In fact, efforts in this direction have even been criticized for placing too much emphasis on process rather than content. Yet, such skills build the foundation of effective citizenship.

These skills are ones in which social studies teachers have typically received little or no training. During the 1980's, we face a situation where the need for the development of such skills has intensified. Increasingly, people find themselves members of groups whose decisions will affect the lives of others. Yet, teachers themselves lack the necessary skills, much less the ability, to teach them to others. School districts will need to assume responsibility for providing the necessary in-service training if the students of the 1980's are to be better prepared than their predecessors to handle group decision making.

PARTICIPATION SKILLS

This last category of skills will overlap with those previously described because participation, or exerting influence in public affairs,[7] includes the skills of decision making, critical thinking, and group effectiveness. At the same time it includes some additional dimensions. In order not to distort the conception of skills developed by Fred Newmann, his list of specific competencies will be presented in totality.

What Are Participation Skills?

Simply stated, participation skills are those competencies that permit citizens to positively influence public affairs. The following specific competencies are suggested:[8]

1. Communicating effectively in spoken and written language.
2. Collecting and logically interpreting information on problems of public concern.
3. Describing political–legal decision-making processes.
4. Rationally justifying personal decisions on controversial public issues and strategies for action with reference to principles of justice and constitutional democracy.
5. Working cooperatively with others.
6. Discussing concrete personal experiences of self and others in ways that contribute to the resolution of personal dilemmas encountered in civic action and that relate these experiences to more general human issues.
7. Using selected technical skills as they are required for exercise of influence on specific issues.

The Significance of Participation Skills

In this section, I will lean heavily on the work of Fred M. Newmann who has been responsible for advancing the thinking of the social studies field in the area of citizen action. Newmann offers three lines of argument that, taken together, constitute a powerful justification for participation skills (the ability to exert influence).

The first of these is a moral argument. In effect, Newmann argues that the ability to exert influence is essential if one is to be a moral agent. Put another way, it is virtually impossible to be moral if one does not have the skills to implement one's decisions. To emphasize the point, Newmann asks us to envision someone who cannot swim, as he or she walks along a deserted beach. Some distance from shore a swimmer is calling for help. The person on the beach is helpless. Because he or she lacks the necessary skills, the moral decision is rendered mute. In effect, lack of competence has cancelled out the individual's moral power.

Second, the ability to influence public affairs fulfills a compelling human need for a sense of efficacy. It builds confidence, reduces anxiety, and contributes to psychological health.

Third, democracy is predicated on the principle of consent of the governed. This principle demands that each citizen have equal opportunity to affect the use of power. In spite of this principle, many citizens (an increasing number) fail to participate. To maximize this democratic principle, to heighten psychological well-being, and to increase the capacity of people to act as moral agents, education for participation skills must be provided.

CONCLUSION

Taken together, the skills discussed in this chapter constitute a most significant foundation for citizen competence in a global age. If even 60 percent of our students develop these competencies by the time they graduate, this democracy will be much stronger and more responsive. Moreover, its people will be more involved and less alienated. Citizenship education has long been a central goal of the public schools. Yet, this goal was only minimally fulfilled in the 1970's.

Clearly, there is much work to be done. New skills have to be learned by students, by teachers, and by those who teach teachers. Resources, time, and expertise need to be provided. The challenge is great, but the cause is critical. The combined efforts of parents, citizens, and educators are needed to ensure that citizen competence for a global age is *the* major educational priority.

REFERENCES

1. Cassidy, Edward W., and Kurfman, Dana G. "Decision Making as Purpose and Process." *Developing Decision-Making Skills.* Forty-Seventh Yearbook of the National Council for the Social Studies. (Edited by Dana G. Kurfman.) Washington, D.C.: the Council, 1977. p. 1.

2. *Ibid.*

3. Phrases within brackets are adaptations made by the author.

4. Cassidy, Edward W., and Kurfman, Dana G. *op. cit.* pp. 19–20.

5. Ennis, Robert H. "A Concept of Critical Thinking: A Proposed Basis for Research in the Teaching and Education of Critical Thinking Ability." *Psychological Concepts in Education.* (Edited by B. Paul Komisar and C.J.B. Macmillan.) Chicago: Rand McNally, 1967. pp. 114–148.

6. Johnson, David W., and Johnson, Frank P. *Joining Together: Group Theory and Group Skills.* Englewood Cliffs, N.J.: Prentice-Hall, 1975. pp. 3–4.

7. Newmann, Fred M.; Bertoici, Thomas A.; and Landsness, Ruthanne M. *Skills in Citizen Action.* Madison, Wisc.: Citizen Participation Curriculum Project, 1977.

8. *Ibid.,* p. 6.

CHAPTER 11

Social Education: A Matter of Values

Beverly J. Armento

As we move through the 1980's we are ever more aware of the *rapidly changing* nature of our world and more conscious of the creative as well as the destructive potentialities of humans. In our most reflective times, surely all of us must contemplate the question, *"What ought to be?"* for ourselves, for our society, for our world. Rapid *change* in the modern world is accompanied by *complexity.* The world is socially complex; our lives may influence and may be influenced by many institutions. Often individuals cannot see how their personal and social lives relate to, influence, and intersect with modern-day institutions. Our lives also may influence and may be influenced by countless individuals—many of whom hold cultural, political, economic, social, and/or religious values different from our own. Often individuals cannot understand "where others are coming from" when they see behavior that is different from their own.

Not only *change* and *social complexity* but also *value complexity* characterizes our time. Social issues are more complex today, partially because issues present a wider variety of choices than in the past. Dealing with more options demands more knowledge of the options and of their consequences. That is difficult because many of the choices for contemporary issues are full of inherent problems and, often, unanticipated consequences.

Thus, today's youth and adults are faced with many questions involving *what ought to be.* The *ought* question is answered as one deals with questions of *valuation*—what is good, bad; what is important, unimportant; what is desirable, undesirable. To better understand our world and to be able to deal effectively with questions of valuation, one must pay prior attention to three areas of concern: (1) What value assumptions and beliefs underlie the behavior of humans and the organization of our social institutions and those institutions of others in the world today? (2) What is important for me? (3) How can I use knowledge and my own values to make well-grounded value decisions in dealing with contemporary personal/social/civic issues?

Can . . . should social education deal with such value-related concerns? Various efforts have been made in the past to focus on value-related goals within social education programs. Some efforts have relegated values education only to the narrow realm of personal choice-making and to interpersonal relationships; some have emphasized a highly analytical approach to value analysis of primarily social issues; some have focused on the development of moral maturity. Each of these emphases is important; but, taken alone (or even in combination), these foci are insufficient if the aim is for a social education program to facilitate effective participation and decision making in the social world. In most cases, the values component of social education programs has been an isolated, add-on part of the curriculum, with little or no relationship made to the on-going, primarily cognitive study of the so-called social world. It seems odd that we have generally embraced a view of the social sciences as a value-free science of humans. This view is an illusion and is one of the major weaknesses of present social education programs.

A three-pronged *integrated* values emphasis is needed for social education programs of the 1980's. (1) Students should learn about the values and beliefs of their own and other cultural groups. In addition, students should be knowledgeable of the value assumptions inherent in American institutions and in those institutions of other countries. (2) As developmentally appropriate, students should acquire values and valuing capabilities. (3) As developmentally appropriate, students should develop the knowledge, affect, and analytic abilities necessary to understand, analyze, and seek more moral solutions to personal, social, and civic value issues.

LEARNING ABOUT CULTURAL AND SOCIAL VALUES

One can neither describe nor understand human behavior or institutions without a consideration of *values.* Values are a fundamental aspect of human striving and an instrinsic part of human life. Values/morality are found in all phases of life: The system of rules and laws, the system for the distribution and allocation of resources, and the kinship system of any particular culture embody and exemplify what is valued, what is important for that particular group of people. Values not only cut through but also define our institutions. The variety in the world of legal, economic, social, and cultural systems is a manifestation of different value systems. To understand the similarities and differences, one must understand the underlying principles. Knowing the underlying value orientations of a group enables one to see the "why" behind human behavior.

To truly understand our own institutions and cultural behaviors, as well as those of other societies, a study of *descriptive values* is needed. An aim would be to acquaint students with the moral and social complexity of the global community and to provide a basis for comprehension, comparison, analysis, and evaluation of individual and group decisions. Such an approach would emphasize an explicit description and analysis of the underlying value assumptions and beliefs that function to guide behavior and decision making through cultures and their institutions.

Values, ideals, and beliefs are feelings and emotions that a person or a group holds. The values themselves are not factual data in the scientific sense; one can neither prove nor disprove them. However, that these value phenomena exist is a scientific fact. Values can be identified, described, catalogued, and compared by using typical scientific procedures. It is in this sense that value data can be viewed as legitimate data of the social sciences.

Granted, some attention has always been directed to the valued reasons for behavior. However, the suggestion here is that this effort be continuous, systematic, and appropriate for the developmental levels of students. That is, the study of "what is" should be combined with the study of "on what it is based." Thus, young children studying about the ways of life of various cultural groups would also learn some of the reasons behind the cultural patterns. Students studying our economic system would learn not only of its workings but also of its assumptions. Any aspect of the "system"—for example, progressive income tax goals and means—could be analyzed in terms of basic value assumptions as well as other, more pragmatic criteria. Studies of comparative economic, political, and social systems would emphasize the "whys." Thus, students should come to seek relationships among human behavior and valued reasons. Students should begin to pause before passing judgment on certain behaviors—to seek the reasons for the behavior; in addition, they should become more aware of the range of value orientations and alternative value solutions to common problems that exist in the world today.

LEARNING ABOUT AND DEVELOPING ONE'S OWN VALUES

Much controversy surrounds this topic. Recently, the "clarifying" and "cognitive developmental" approaches to values/moral education brought with them many interesting instructional materials and teaching techniques. They also brought much misunderstanding, misinterpretation, and legitimate concern over the role, rights, and responsibilities of schools to deal with the development of values. This is not the appropriate place for a full analysis of the issues; let us be aware, however, that this goal area demands our most serious attention in the coming decade.

"What is important for me?" The answers to this question for each of us change over time; the answers are strongly influenced by our cultural and religious beliefs, and by the particular events of our early childhoods. We are influenced—overtly or covertly—by our family, friends, teachers, schooling, and other social experiences to value certain behaviors and beliefs—and to disvalue others. If nothing else, school experiences transmit a hidden value agenda through curriculum choices and through systems of rewards and punishments. If we relegate values education to the "hidden curriculum," we have opted for indoctrination. Surely the transmission of a particular set of values for all persons is not a viable or morally appropriate posture, given the pluralistic nature of our society and of the world and the serious need for intelligent citizens in the world today.

Schools have a special responsibility to help preserve the rights of students, families, and cultural groups to privacy and to the preservation of their cultural/religious values. However, schools also have a particular responsibility to individuals to facilitate the development of the intellect, of reasoned thought and behavior. It is to this end that social education programs should strive. Intelligence enables one to reflectively decide upon value-goals and to seek appropriate means for attaining these goals. Schools can facilitate the development of "informed," as opposed to "borrowed," values. Borrowed values come from outside the person, are absorbed from significant others, and are taken on without consideration of alternatives. This is the pattern of value learning in early childhood. However, as children gain logical–analytical skills, they should learn about and apply the *process* of valuing. As this occurs, values and moral precepts are more consciously constructed by the learner.

116

Schools can also promote a respect for and an appreciation of value discourse itself and the range of value alternatives to many of life's questions. Students should come to see that for many aspects of life (such as values of beauty, values of personal preference), there are many legitimate choices—all acceptable in many societies.

USING VALUES AND ANALYTIC SKILLS

In this rapidly changing, socially and ethically complex world, the social education curriculum must express concern not only for *what is happening* in the social world but also for *what ought to be happening*. What are the changes doing *to* and *for* humans? Are the changes desirable, good, and preferred? The future of our form of government depends upon the capacity of future generations to deal effectively, thoughtfully, humanely, and rationally with decision making in all aspects of the social world—politically, economically, ecologically, socially. To understand, analyze, and make personal decisions on personal/social/ civic issues demands knowledge, skill, affect, and clarity of valued goals. Affect or desire to participate in on-going decision-making processes in one's community or one's nation is a part of social education that we have neglected. Two-thirds of all eligible voters typically don't vote in national elections; many persons feel ineffective in influencing changes in the political or economic systems. This aspect of values education demands our concern and our creative solutions.

Knowledge is needed by students as they deal with social issues. In this age of complexity, considerable background data are needed before any rational value analysis can be conducted on an issue. In some previous efforts within the social studies, emphasis was placed on developing the *process* of value analysis independently of content.

Certainly analytic procedures are essential to the development of effective decision making. Somehow, we must strive to educate students to apply thoughtful processes—along with the necessary data and their own value preferences—to the intelligent analysis of social/civic issues. Social education curriculums could present model examples of different kinds of issues—presenting exemplar analyses for the teacher as well as the student. Issues dealt with in classrooms would be more complex and difficult as students developmentally were more able to deal with them. With a systematic approach to value analysis, perhaps more of our graduating seniors could understand, assess, and take action on important issues.

In summary, a values emphasis within the social education program should seek to *educate* (rather than indoctrinate) students (1) about val-

117

ues that exist in the world today and that influence, in a major way, human behavior and group choices; (2) about their own values and about the methods humans employ to seek valued goals; and (3) about the reasons, knowledge, and skills necessary for dealing effectively with serious social/civic issues.

CHAPTER 12

Societal Forces and the Social Studies

Stanley P. Wronski

In the 1950's, during a Senate committee hearing on organized crime in the United States, a reputed mobster was asked a rather accusatory question by the committee counsel. His response was, "I refuse to answer on the basis of the Fifth Amendment to the Constitution, which protects me from self-incriminatory statements." When asked by counsel where he learned to give such a response, he answered smilingly, "I learned it by watching TV." This sardonic reply clearly illustrates the fact that all of us accumulate knowledge about our society from sources other than the social studies curriculum in schools.

As we survey the range of problems facing the American citizen in the 1980's and beyond, we social studies teachers might well ask a similar type of question: What and where will our students—elementary, secondary, and adult—learn about the major social issues of our time?

It is a relatively simple matter to get information on *what* people think about various contemporary issues; the national opinion polls—Gallup, Roper, Harris, and others—report this periodically. Even among young adults and teen-agers we are able to obtain a fairly reliable indication of their thinking through such special surveys as those conducted by *Scholastic* magazine and the Institute for Social Research. For example, a recent Institute for Social Research poll indicated that 41 percent of college freshmen believe that both large corporations and major labor unions have "considerable dishonesty/immorality."[1]

It is not so simple a matter to get information on *where* people obtain their information about social issues. The reasons for this difficulty are numerous and beyond the scope of this chapter: Ferreting out such information is frequently seen as an unacceptable invasion of privacy; the subject may not recall his or her source of information; or the subject may be genuinely mistaken in identifying a source. But the importance of inquiring into the source of people's information on social issues relates directly to the raison d'être of the social studies.

If *all* of the students' knowledge about society can be obtained from sources other than formal schooling, why should there be such an entity as the social studies curriculum? If, however, *some* of their knowledge comes via their social studies courses in school, it behooves us to inquire into the nature and source of this knowledge. Such inquiry should help us to establish at least some rough "turf" boundaries so that we can determine what kinds of social food crops we can deliberately plant and cultivate, and what kinds we should leave to the surrounding natural environment. The ideal goal is to achieve some kind of symbiotic relationship between the cultivated (formal schooling) and the natural (nonformal education) environments.

SOURCES OF SOCIAL LEARNING

For purposes of establishing a framework for inquiring into this educational symbiosis, three representative types of social issues are identified—the energy crises, problems involving international relations, and problems involving interpersonal behavior. These are by no means intended to encompass the entire range of possible issues, but they are chosen because they meet criteria for the selection of problems for intensive social study: (1) they are of current and long-range significance; (2) they are of relatively high interest to students; (3) they involve normative judgments; and (4) they are each susceptible to a wide range of plausible solutions.

For each of the above three broad types of issues, a subset of three questions can be raised: These inquire into the *source* of the student's (1) knowledge, (2) attitudes, and (3) decision-making skills associated with each issue. In tabular form, the analytical scheme is depicted in Figure 1.

While this scheme contains hypothetical responses, it is possible to obtain some actual data on these and similar social issues.

In an attempt to get such data on the sources of information held

FIGURE 1
A SCHEME FOR ANALYZING REPRESENTATIVE SOCIAL ISSUES

Nature & Source / Issue	Student *knowledge* of the issue	Where obtained	Student *attitude* toward the issue	Where obtained	Student *decision-making ability* re the issue	Where obtained
I. Energy crisis	Gasoline/oil shortages	TV, newspapers, magazines, school	Places primary blame on OPEC	Parents	Feels the U.S. should use military force to obtain energy	Discussions with peers
II. International relations	Economic dependency of developing nations on industrialized nations	TV special on Africa	Is sympathetic to plight of developing nations	Exchange students	Favors implementing New International Economic Order	Inquiry exercises in school
III. Interpersonal behavior	Extent of venereal disease in the U.S.	Public service advertisements	Exhibits confusion and ambivalence	Peers and advice columns	Says "Let the chips fall"	Personal introspection

by students on social issues, this author administered a rather simple Social Inventory Scale to a random sample of college students. It should be stressed that the instrument is in no way intended to be a completely refined, pretested, and validated poll. The results, while not pretending to be statistically sophisticated, may have some heuristic value. They suggest that nonschool sources make a major contribution to young adults' knowledge, attitudes, and decision-making ability (see Figure 2).

The Social Inventory Scale dealt with the three representative categories of social issues mentioned above—energy, international relations, and interpersonal relations. The responses to only one of these, the energy issue, are summarized in Figure 2. Responses to the other two issues reveal a similar pattern. For purposes of this analysis, perhaps the most revealing information is that the majority of respondents indicate that they obtained *little* or *nothing* in the way of knowledge, attitudes, or decision-making ability from their elementary and secondary school experiences.

FIGURE 2

Sources of Knowledge, Attitudes, and Decision-Making Ability on the Energy Issue Among a Random Sample of College Students [in percentages (N = 143)]

A. Indicate to what extent, in your estimation, the following contributed to your *knowledge* about the energy issue.

PERCENTAGES OF RESPONSES

SOURCE	Not at all	Little	Moderately	Largely	Exclusively
1. TV newscasts	3	8	37	50	2
2. TV specials	12	27	36	24	1
3. Newspaper news coverage	1	23	38	37	1
4. Newspaper opinion pages	28	35	28	8	1
5. News magazines	8	33	32	25	2
6. Other journals	38	38	15	9	0
7. Parents and family	11	28	34	23	4
8. Friends and peers	17	44	36	1	2
9. Elementary school classes	76	18	6	0	0
10. Secondary school classes	45	25	24	5	1
11. College-level classes	20	25	26	25	4

B. Indicate to what extent, in your estimation, the following contributed to your present *attitudes* toward the energy issue.

1. TV newscasts	4	16	36	40	4
2. TV specials	15	25	28	29	3
3. Newspaper news coverage	8	29	31	27	5
4. Newspaper opinion pages	36	36	20	8	0
5. News magazines	16	35	26	23	0
6. Other journals	53	33	5	9	0
7. Parents and family	17	20	23	34	6
8. Friends and peers	17	23	31	25	4
9. Elementary school classes	82	14	4	0	0
10. Secondary school classes	58	24	14	3	1
11. College-level classes	22	26	23	25	4

FIGURE 2 (Continued)

C. Indicate to what extent, in your estimation, the following contributed to your *ability to make decisions* relating to the energy issue (e.g., to decide to ride a bicycle rather than drive a car to school, to engage in a boycott or demonstration, etc.)

PERCENTAGES OF RESPONSES

SOURCE	Not at all	Little	Moderately	Largely	Exclusively
1. TV newscasts	12	23	42	22	1
2. TV specials	20	28	36	15	1
3. Newspaper news coverage	14	29	32	23	2
4. Newspaper opinion pages	39	33	22	6	0
5. News magazines	23	30	27	19	1
6. Other journals	48	32	12	6	2
7. Parents and family	15	24	23	32	6
8. Friends and peers	16	26	30	25	3
9. Elementary school classes	79	17	3	1	0
10. Secondary school classes	54	30	12	3	1
11. College-level classes	32	23	20	22	3

The results obtained in the above survey, however imprecise the instrument, seem to support the position taken by Donald Warren in his analysis of the influence of societal forces on the social learning of youth. After dealing with such influences as the Americanization of immigrants, job training, and social mobility, he writes:

It is fair to conclude that the public school has enjoyed mixed success in socializing American youth. Its roles have been limited and its effectiveness curtailed by other, sometimes more powerful, institutions and forces. Clearly, the school has not been the only, or even always the dominant, educational process available to the young. It is incapable, alone, of preparing them for adulthood. Furthermore, its effectiveness has been frequently undermined by patterns of exclusion and inequality reflecting both school policies and social practice. At best, the public school remains as a promise, however faulty in construction and incomplete in delivery, that the proper preparation of the young is a matter of public concern and commitment.[2]

SCHOOL RESPONSES TO SOCIETAL FORCES

What can social studies teachers do about the fact that a substantial amount of our knowledge about social issues is derived from sources other than the school. First and most importantly, they can recognize and accept it. Like other self-evident truths, however, this situation is more easily stated than internalized. Many teachers still have pangs of conscience when they contemplate the amount of curricular material they *intended* to cover in their course in comparison to what they were actually able to do. This syndrome tends to afflict teachers especially in May or June of the school year.

In the interest of pedagogical realism and personal peace of mind, teachers need to rid themselves of the nagging guilt feeling about not having "covered all the material." Is it really imperative that students recall the provisions of the Missouri Compromise or all of President Wilson's Fourteen Points? This is not said to encourage indolence or indifference on the part of teachers, but rather to drive home the point that no teacher in any course can possibly cover all the material in that subject.

Besides merely accepting the fact that out-of-school social learning does, indeed, take place, social studies teachers can actively utilize non-school phenomena to complement and enhance the social studies curriculum. Examples of such potential utilization are especially abundant in (1) public television, (2) commercial television, and (3) print media.

Fortunately for teachers, many television stations affiliated with the Public Broadcasting Service offer excellent programs which can provide a new dimension to classroom and textbook studies. Among the outstanding fare distributed by PBS are *Masterpiece Theatre, National Geographic* specials, historical dramatizations such as *I, Claudius,* and kaleidoscopic series such as *Connections,* in which each program is an integrated lesson in history, the humanities, science, and social science.

Commercial television, despite its outpouring of programs with little redeeming social value, still manages to come up with a gem now and then. Some of the best of these are selected by Prime Time School Television (PTST) as especially suited for viewing by students. PTST then produces instructional guides relating to these programs, intended for teacher and student use. Among the programs for which it has already prepared guides are *Roots, Einstein's Universe,* and *Edward the King.*

Despite the glamour of television and its associated electronic components, the printed word remains a powerful and significant means for communicating messages about the human condition. Perhaps the most ubiquitous example of the mass media is the daily newspaper. Often cursed and occasionally derided—and frequently the justifiable recipient of both—the newspaper is still a powerful ally that can be used by imaginative social studies teachers. Teachers who are fortunate enough to have access to a good daily newspaper in the community may use it to supplement, enliven, and reify social studies subject matter. Even the teacher with a poor newspaper in the community can use it to educational advantage by having the students discover and critically analyze biased reporting, unequal coverage, omissions, slanted headlines, and various propaganda devices.

Besides mass media, there are other all-pervasive social forces in our midst that social studies teachers can use to powerful advantage. They consist of the various social institutions in which we are all, to a greater or lesser extent, immersed. Of particular significance are our patterns of behavior and beliefs with respect to our economic system, political system, family, and religion. Collectively, they define our culture. As the anthropologist Ralph Linton observed, probably the last thing a fish would think of investigating is the water in which it is constantly immersed. Humans, at least, have the *potential* of intellectually detaching themselves from their environment and observing it as a visitor from outer space would. Young adults, in particular, are often surprised when they realize that not all economic systems are based on profit-making, that political leadership may reside in collectivities as well as in individuals, that the extended family rather than the nuclear family is the prevalent pattern among more than half of the world's population, and that not all religions are monotheistic.

Thus far, in considering the utilization of nonschool phenomena, we have dealt mainly with the substance or subject matter to be learned. What about the *process* by which learning takes place? In the past, this topic was the almost exclusive domain of educators, psychologists, and other academicians. Various advocates place differing amounts of emphasis on such rubrics of learning as stimulus–response, gestalt, operant conditioning, problem solving, and the like. These stem largely from psychological theory. What about learning that stems from *social* realities?

The most recent Club of Rome study explores a wide range of aspects of the learning process that go beyond the traditional educational systems. The contributors to *No Limits to Learning: Bridging the Human Gap*[3] identify two types of learning: *participatory* and *anticipatory*. Participatory learning deals with the interplay of social forces, values, images, and human relations in the learning process. Anticipatory learning deals with the capacity to be proactive rather than only reactive to the current of events. Participatory learning occurs, for example, when a local business firm, in order to avoid bankruptcy, agrees to share its decision-making authority with its employees. In a situation such as this, an entirely new set of accommodations, modifications, concessions, perspectives, relationships, and priorities—in short, participatory learning—is achieved. Anticipatory learning is exemplified by the formulation of a comprehensive national plan to meet energy demands *before* the present nonrenewable energy sources are exhausted or severely depleted.

In both participatory and anticipatory learning situations, the learning mode is dependent mainly upon forces outside the school. This reciprocal relationship between social events and social learning may necessitate a fundamental rethinking on the part of many social studies teachers that is akin to the Copernican revolution in astronomy. Many teachers have assumed that their primary goal is to develop a kind of abstract "ability to think" in their students. With this at the center, so the argument goes, the students can resolve the many complex problems, both social and personal, that revolve about them. What the Club of Rome study suggests is that the starting point for learning, especially in the social studies, resides in contemporary societal problems. With these at the center, the learner uses various peripheral learning processes —participatory, anticipatory, traditional, or a combination of these.

If the above analysis of the Club of Rome study has any validity, it suggests that the social studies curriculum can not only *accept* and *utilize* the social forces that impinge upon it but also, in a modest way, even *modify* them. This is said neither to delude nor to exaggerate. It can be inferred that without a rudimentary understanding of American traditions and values, gained to some extent in social studies classes, there would have occurred neither leadership nor followership in such significant American social actions as the anti-war protest of the 1960's, the consumer awareness movement of the 1970's, and the emerging consciousness of global perspectives of the 1980's.

SYMBIOSIS

We are now full circle. In an attempt to understand the future of the social studies, we have been forced to reflect on the past and how that has been modified by the countervailing forces of continuity and change. Perhaps this relationship can best be depicted in diagrammatic form (see Figure 3).

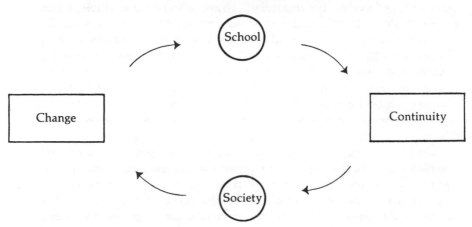

FIGURE 3

A MODEL OF THE RELATIONSHIP BETWEEN SCHOOL AND SOCIETY

School

Change

Continuity

Society

According to this circular flow model of the educational process, there exists a systemic relationship between school and society—a social symbiosis. The predominant direction of the flow is clockwise. The typical social studies curriculum in most schools—in the United States and elsewhere—is literally conservative in that it transmits a body of information and values designed to reinforce and continue the polity. This original package of beliefs and attitudes might be, and usually is, modified by the social realities encountered by the learner in the course of a lifetime. Over the years, some of these modified positions might be, and frequently are, institutionalized by law or custom. This modified cultural pattern is then reinforced through the schools.

A specific example can be used to illustrate the model in action. In the United States during the 1920's and early 1930's, most schools glorified the rugged individualism of our economic system, especially in their social studies curriculums. But this conservative view was severely challenged by the Great Depression of the 1930's. As a result of New Deal legislation and World War II, tremendous social changes occurred —e.g., the growth of unionism, Social Security, concern about East– West relations, etc. These societal changes, in turn, became an essential part of the post-World-War-II curriculums.

It should be noted that it is *possible* for schooling to exert influence in a counterclockwise direction. According to the reconstructionist theory of education, this *should* be the way in which the schools contribute directly to bringing about social change. Working from a blueprint for social reconstruction, the schools would actively promote such goals as economic security and international peace. But even the most ardent defenders of this theory admit that it has found relatively little popular support in the United States.

Realistically, for the 1980's most social studies teachers will find themselves filling a role described by Bismarck when he observed that we cannot create the current of events; we can only float with it and steer. But within that role there is considerable leeway. One can adopt a relatively conservative stance and roll with the waves. One can, even within Bismarck's context, engage students in participatory and anticipatory learning experiences. Or, departing from tradition, one can say, "I am the captain of my ship," and actively work and steer with students toward the direct achievement of social changes.

REFERENCES

1. Bachman, Jerald G., and Johnston, Lloyd D. *Fewer Rebels, Fewer Causes: A Profile of Today's College Freshmen.* Monitoring the Future, Occasional Paper 4. Ann Arbor, Mich.: Institute for Social Research, 1979.

2. Warren, Donald R. "A Proper Preparation: Historical Perspectives on Schools and Socialization in America." *From Youth to Constructive Adult Life: The Role of the Public School.* (Edited by Ralph W. Tyler.) Berkeley, Calif.: McCutchan Publishing, 1978. p. 13.

3. Botkin, James W.; Elmandjra, Mahdi; and Malitza, Mircea. *No Limits to Learning: Bridging the Human Gap.* Oxford: Pergamon Press, 1979. pp. 24–33.

CHAPTER 13

Teachers for the Social Studies

Charles B. Myers

Just prior to the start of the 1980's, two questions about schools seemed to pervade both public and scholarly literature on education: (1) How good are the schools? (2) What is good and bad about them? In general, both opinionnaires and research data produced mixed reviews and mixed results. In a national poll of American citizens in 1979, parents of school-age children were asked, "What do you like most about the school your child attends?" The most frequent response was, "Its good teachers." When all those polled were asked, "What are the main things a school has to do before it can earn an 'A' grade?" the largest number answered, "Improve the quality of teachers." The same poll showed, however, that only 34 percent of Americans would give schools an "A" or "B" grade, compared with 48 percent in 1974. It also indicated that 85 percent of Americans approve of state examinations for teachers as they begin teaching and every few years while in the profession.[1]

During the 1970's educational research studies that sought to determine the factors that affect how much and how well students learn indicated that no single factor was clearly the main determinant, but a broad reading of the findings leaves the distinct impression that teachers are at least one of the most critical variables.[2] These studies state that the subject matter taught, school organization and size, nature of the local community, amount of funds expended, and student family background all affect learning. They also show that what happens in the specific school and classroom of a student is significantly important. In effect, the studies show two types of factors—those external to schools and to the learning process and those internal to both. Since the external factors are most difficult to change, factors related directly to schools and the learning process become the most important variables in attempting to improve student learning. If this is true, those who control these factors—that is, factors that can be modified relatively easily—will determine most significantly how well students learn. More than anyone else, teachers have a greater ability to influence these factors.

In very general terms, public thinking and educational research at the beginning of the 1980's seem to be saying at least two things concerning teachers, schools, and the American public: (1) Teachers are considered the critical factor in determining what students learn, and (2) Americans have high expectations about the quality of their schools. Since these conditions, which are valid for social studies teachers as well as for their colleagues, are not expected to change during the 1980's, the quality of the performance of social studies teachers between 1980 and 1990 will be considered the primary determinant of what social studies students do or do not learn.

But social studies teachers do not function in a vacuum, and while the importance of teachers will continue and the high level of expectation placed upon them will remain throughout the decade, we also know that—

1. School-age children learn much more from television and other media than they learn from planned classroom instruction.

2. More money is spent on media presentations, such as *Roots, Holocaust,* and *Sesame Street,* than on materials traditionally designed for the classroom.

3. Each year, business and industry in the United States spend more money for training their personnel than is spent on the in-service education of teachers.

4. Corporations usually train and retrain their employees on paid company time but school systems do so only rarely.

5. Inflation and energy costs are diverting money away from instructional expenses in school budgets.

6. Proportionally fewer new teachers are finding jobs in the profession.

7. Teacher "burn out" and stress have become so common that they are written about in the popular press.

So, what does this all mean for social studies teachers of the 1980's? What will our lives be like for these 10 years? In which directions will we move as individuals and as a profession? The remaining pages of this chapter attempt to answer these questions in three contexts: (1) the world of the 1980's in general, (2) the social studies field of the 1980's, and (3) the teaching profession of the 1980's. In each context, we can look at some assumptions and expectations about the decade, and relate them to our lives as teachers and to the lives of the children we teach.

SOCIAL STUDIES TEACHERS AND THE WORLD OF THE 1980's

Of course, life in the 1980's will continue to become increasingly complex. Change will continue to accelerate. World, national, and local events will have sudden and intense impact on teachers, students, and instruction. Schools and teachers will be caught in the cross-currents and conflicting pressures of the times.

Social studies teachers will face more and louder demands for perfection as citizen and parent expectations of schools rise even higher. They will feel the brunt of criticism as frustrations with life's complex problems overwhelm citizens who have always turned to the schools to prepare themselves and their children for productive, happy lives.

Citizens who, in the 1970's, complained about weaknesses in reading, writing, and arithmetic instruction will turn more of their attention to social studies. History, geography, civics, and practical economics will come under particularly strong pressure and close parent and taxpayer inspection. The back-to-basics movement, which social studies educators felt neglected their field in the 1970's, will turn its attention to social studies and will demand an accounting. Low student test scores in the traditional social studies areas will be decried publicly.

Although the old idea that parents turn their children over to the schools to be taught as the educators see fit is a thing of the past, parents and the general society will continue to expect teachers and schools to raise the children in those areas where the home and other social institutions seem to be the weakest. Social studies teachers still will be expected to eliminate bigotry, enable students to get along with each other, improve student understanding of complex economic issues, explain cultural differences, interpret religious traditions, instill love and respect of country, undergird the Judeo-Christian values of Western civilization, prepare students to "fit in" in a chaotic world, and develop citizenship and vocational skills. But none of these expectations is new. Society has looked to schools, and particularly the social studies classroom, for years for the difficult task of socializing its children and youth. What might be different, however, is the number and complexity of the tasks placed at the classroom door.

The demands and expectations will be burdensome, possibly overwhelming, but not unfair. They will be directed toward social studies teachers because what social studies teachers do is so important. During the 80's Americans will come to realize that importance more than ever before.

THE SOCIAL STUDIES OF THE 1980's

Since the content of the social studies of the 80's has been discussed in earlier chapters, only a few general observations about the relationship between content and social studies teachers are in order here. It appears that social studies teachers throughout the decade will continue to face at least three persistent dilemmas involving their subject matter. One focuses on the question of which social studies areas to stress. The second concerns questions of teaching approach and style. The third involves two parts: first, how to select from the avalanche of information being generated in each social science field the material that is appropriate for elementary and secondary school students, and, second, how to transfer that information into a form appropriate for day-to-day classroom instruction.

Put simply, as the 1980's began, social scientists, historians, and social studies educators did not "have their act together," and the confusion can be expected to remain through the decade.[3] Disciplinarians in each social science field will still demand more time in the curriculum and more space in instructional materials for their specific areas of interest. Prominent social studies educators will continue their appeals of the 1970's for concept, generalization, values-based instruction that incorporates humanistic, urban, and global thrusts. Others will demand a return to a more basic history, geography, civics, and factual curriculum. Although the advocates for more traditional content will gain prominence during the decade, the conflicts will not fade. As a result, social studies faculties will continue to face the difficult and often personal choices of selecting which subjects to teach and which materials to use. They will have to do so as the scholars and local pressure groups continue to express ideas and demands that are diverse and often mutually exclusive.

132

Debates about teaching approach and style will continue to burden social studies teachers through the decade. Researchers and college professors will still call for inquiry teaching, high-level questioning, multicultural classroom environments, values analysis, and so forth. More traditional spokespersons and textbook publishers will require a return to more "basic" instruction.[4] In addition, analyzers of teacher and classroom behavior will suggest new and more complex ways for social studies teachers to improve their "act." They will provide, for example, more sophisticated ideas on teaching and learning styles, teacher–student verbal interaction patterns, and anthropological analyses of the classroom.[5] Teachers will not be able to assimilate all the ideas, however, because mechanisms to synthesize the ideas and to transform them into usable classroom practice will still be lacking through most of the decade.

As has been the case in recent years, the information developed in each subject field within the social studies will increase in geometric fashion. As it does, teachers, curriculum committees, authors, and publishers—after they determine what subject to cover at which grade level —will have to decide more critically what to stress within each subject area, what to treat lightly, and what to ignore. The problem will not be different in kind from the past, but it will be more difficult because so much more will have to be left untaught and such large chunks of information will not be covered. It will also be more difficult because the new information will be more technical and more precise and, therefore, harder to make understandable to young students. This will happen, of course, as pressures on teachers increase to teach more to their students and to teach it better—as "accountability" and test scores pervade all formal education.

THE TEACHING PROFESSION OF THE 1980's

The teaching profession evolved into maturity during the 1970's, and, as an organized entity, it will affect the professional lives of social studies teachers in the 1980's more than ever before. The profession's sophistication and persistent influence will be obvious throughout the decade at all levels of education and educational policy making—in schools, school districts, state capitals, and Washington. For many social studies teachers, there will be a new-found source of support and, at times, a sorely needed refuge. Social studies teachers will rely on the teaching profession for direction, for power, for a sense of belonging, and for defensive assistance. They will seek advice and guidance from the profession in policy formation, in curriculum decision making, in professional development, and in the more personal realms of financial well-being and job security.

Social studies teachers will turn to the teaching profession because they will face continued inflation at home, reduced financial support for schools, and an oversupplied job market. The roles expected of them will continue to be confused. At times they will be unappreciated. Students will be harder to "reach." Pressures for improved achievement test results will escalate. School bureaucracies will be harder to tolerate. Teachers will be under more stress. They will be getting older as a group. They will be absent from the classroom more frequently. They will "burn out" more often and earlier.

At the same time, social studies teachers will be the best educated, the most skilled, and, probably, the most dedicated in history. They will learn more in their preservice education than did their pre-1980 counterparts. They will continue their education through in-service programs throughout their careers. A larger percentage will complete advanced degrees, and more of this advanced work will be more appropriate to their classroom responsibilities than in the past. By 1990 many, if not most, teachers will have attained the doctoral degree or its equivalent.[6]

The concept and philosophy of teacher centers will continue to develop during the decade, and, if the many teacher centers already established begin to bear fruit, the center concept and the idea of teacher-controlled in-service education will provide new opportunities for teacher self-development. The future of these ideas is not at all secure, however. Political battles over "the governance issue" will remain, and the teacher center movement must avoid pitfalls that lurk ahead. It must avoid the fad and lack-of-impact-on-the-classroom fate that befell many National Science Foundation Institutes, Triple T Projects, and Teacher Corps efforts of earlier decades. Specific program activities and goals will have to be assessed constantly for their appropriateness to teachers and students, for their quality and focus of instruction, and for their ability to be criticized, modified, and improved. The real test of the the viability of the teacher center concept will come during the decade when federal government funds to specific centers end. The key questions are: Will they be valuable enough to continue without subsidy? If they do not continue, what will replace them as the primary mechanism for teacher staff development?

Social studies teachers, as part of the teaching profession, will have more power and control over the quality and direction of their professional lives in the 1980's than most educators anticipated only a few years ago. How well we handle that responsibility and how we join forces with colleges, school administrators, and the general public to continue to serve America's children and youth are up to us. Possibilities for greatly improved social studies instruction, for failure, and for continued drift will all exist.

CONCLUSIONS

Social studies teachers of the 1980's will face more difficult challenges than their predecessors. The times will be more complex. Society will expect more. Students will be more complex, more diverse, and more confused. The subject matter will be more cluttered with information and more intricate ideas. The teaching profession will be more powerful and more responsible for its own destiny. Teachers, individually and as a group, will be more sophisticated, better educated, and more able to continue their education.

Under these circumstances, will we be more successful than we have been in the past in educating America's children and youth to become better citizens and better human beings? We certainly *can* be. We can be—if we retain the same commitment to our goals and to the success of our students that we have always possessed; if we continue to study our fields; if we continue to analyze our complex world and impose some degree of intellectual order on it; if we continue to assume, assess, and adjust the ever-changing roles that are thrust upon us as teachers; if we keep looking ahead; if we continue to set our own professional directions; and if we work together as the professionals that we are.

In 1990, as in 1980 and previous decades, social studies teachers will be the critical determinant in the learning process of social studies students. How good we are at our profession will determine how much and how well our students learn. What really happens in our social studies classrooms and in the minds and lives of our students is up to us.

REFERENCES

1. *Phi Delta Kappan,* September 1979. pp. 33–45.

2. For example, see: Averch, Harvey A., and others. *A Rand Educational Policy Study: How Effective Is Schooling? A Critical Review of Research.* Englewood Cliffs, N.J.: Educational Technology Publications, 1974.

Berman, Paul, and others. *Federal Programs Supporting Educational Change.* Santa Monica, Calif.: Rand Corp., 1975. 5 vols.

Jarolimek, John, editor. "The Status of Social Studies Education: Six Case Studies." *Social Education* 41: 574–601; November–December 1977.

Gross, Richard E. "The Status of the Social Studies in the Public Schools of the United States: Facts and Impressions of a National Survey." *Social Education* 41: 194–200, 205; March 1977.

Shaver, James P.; Davis, O.L., Jr.; and Helburn, Suzanne W. "The Status of Social Studies Education: Impressions from Three NSF Studies." *Social Education* 43: 150–153; February 1979.

Senesh, Lawrence. "Social Competence: A Challenge for Teacher Training." *The Social Studies* 69: 3–6; January–February 1978.

3. As one illustration of this confusion, see: *Education USA* 21; December 4, 1978.

4. See: Schneider, Donald O., and VanSickle, Ronald L. "The Status of the Social Studies: The Publishers' Perspective." *Social Education* 41: 461–465; October 1979.

5. Studies of these types are being conducted, for example, by Beverly Armento at Georgia State University, Mary Friend Sheppard at Indiana University, and Jane J. White at the University of Maryland at Baltimore.

6. Lawrence A. Cremin addressed the continuing education of teachers thoughtfully in "The Education of the Educating Professions," The Nineteenth Hunt Lecture of the American Association of Colleges for Teacher Education, Chicago, 1978. (Copies are available from AACTE.)

Jack Allen is Professor of History Emeritus, George Peabody College for Teachers of Vanderbilt University. A past president of the National Council for the Social Studies (1958), he has published widely in the social studies, including textbooks and other instructional materials at the elementary and secondary levels, professional books, yearbooks, and periodicals. He has held positions with a number of national educational organizations and has served as a social studies consultant to school systems and universities in the United States and other countries.

Beverly J. Armento is Associate Professor of Social Studies Education, Georgia State University. She has served as an elementary school teacher and/or curriculum consultant in the public schools of New Jersey, Florida, Maryland, Indiana, Georgia, New Mexico, and Hawaii. She has also held responsible positions with national organizations in the fields of social studies, teacher education, and educational research.

Phillip Bacon is Professor of Geography, University of Houston. A past president of the National Council for Geographic Education (1966), he was recipient of the Council's Distinguished Service Award in 1974. He is a member of the Council and Chair, Publications Committee, Association of American Geographers. Professor Bacon received the University of Houston's Teaching Excellence Award in 1975 and again in 1979. His wide range of publications includes textbooks and other instructional materials and editorship of the 1970 Yearbook of the National Council for the Social Studies.

Barry K. Beyer is Professor of Education and Coordinator of the Doctor of Arts in Education program at George Mason University in Fairfax, Virginia. Formerly a secondary school social studies teacher and department chairperson, he has written extensively on social studies curriculum and instruction. He has served as Chair of the Publications Board, National Council for the Social Studies, and as a consultant to more than fifty universities and public school systems in the United States and Ghana. His latest books are *Teaching Thinking in Social Studies* (1979) and *Back-to-Basics in Social Studies* (1977).

Lynn A. Fontana is Research Assistant, Social Studies Development Center, Indiana University. She has taught in the public schools of New Jersey and Pennsylvania, and served as Program Assistant at the Educational Testing Service, Princeton. She holds the Ph.D. in Social Studies Education from Indiana University.

Richard E. Gross is Professor, School of Education, Stanford University. A past president of the National Council for the Social Studies (1967), he has had a distinguished career as a social studies teacher in Wisconsin, as a university professor in Florida and California, and as a guest professor in Wales, Germany, and Australia. Professor Gross has served as curriculum consultant to schools in a number of states and to a Pilot Schools Project in Spain. His publications cover a broad range in school social studies, social studies education, and the history and sociology of education.

Carole L. Hahn is Associate Professor, Division of Educational Studies, Emory University. She has taught social studies in junior and senior high schools, and has worked with curriculum diffusion projects. Among her numerous national professional activities are membership on the Board of Directors of the National Council for the Social Studies; Chair of the Council's Publication Board; and Secretary–Treasurer of the Special Interest Group: Social Studies of the American Educational Research Association. Dr. Hahn has directed a number of funded projects, most recently a Career Education project funded by the U.S. Office of Education.

John Jarolimek is Professor of Education and Associate Dean for Undergraduate Studies and Teacher Education, College of Education, University of Washington. A past president of the National Council for the Social Studies (1971), his significant educational contributions include service as elementary school teacher and principal, university professor, and educational consultant. His numerous professional publications include *Social Studies in Elementary Education,* currently in its fifth edition, and textbooks for the elementary school.

Howard D. Mehlinger is Professor of Education and History, and Director of the Social Studies Development Center, Indiana University. A past president of the National Council for the Social Studies (1977), he is a recognized leader in citizenship education in the United States and Europe. Prior to his university service, he was, for a decade, a high school social studies teacher in Lawrence, Kansas. Professor Mehlinger is actively involved as an educational writer, consultant, and publishing advisor.

Charles L. Mitsakos is Assistant Superintendent of Schools for Curriculum and Instruction, Andover, Massachusetts. A former social studies classroom teacher and supervisor, he is the author of numerous instructional materials for both elementary and secondary schools. He has worked extensively in the United States and abroad in social studies education and curriculum development.

Charles B. Myers is Professor of History and Social Studies Education, and Chair, Department of Teaching and Learning, George Peabody College for Teachers of Vanderbilt University. A former junior high school social studies teacher and educational innovator in Pennsylvania, he is active nationally as a curriculum consultant and member of the Board of Directors, National Council for the Social Studies. His publications include authorship and editing of textbooks in elementary social studies and a variety of professional articles.

Anna S. Ochoa is Associate Professor of Social Studies Education, School of Education, Indiana University. A past president of the National Council for the Social Studies (1978), she is nationally recognized as a speaker, consultant, and author. She has had elementary school teaching experience and has, among her writings, co-authorship of a textbook series in elementary social studies.

138

Dorothy J. Skeel is Professor of Social Studies Education, George Peabody College for Teachers of Vanderbilt University. She has been a public school teacher on the elementary and secondary levels, and a faculty member at Indiana University. An author and consultant for textbooks in elementary school social studies, her most recent professional publication is *The Challenge of Teaching Social Studies in the Elementary School,* Third edition.

Stanley P. Wronski is Professor of Education and Social Science, College of Education, Michigan State University. A past president of the National Council for the Social Studies (1974), he has been active in the social studies movement at the local, state, and national levels in the United States and in curriculum development in Thailand. As a writer, he is particularly well known for his co-authorship (with Edgar B. Wesley) of *Teaching Secondary Social Studies in a World Society,* Sixth edition.